Adobe Creative Cloud 2018

Introduction to InDesign, Photoshop, & Illustrator

Learn by doing step by step exercises.

Includes downloadable class files that work on Mac & PC.

EDITION 1.1

Published by:
Noble Desktop
594 Broadway, Suite 1202
New York, NY 10012
nobledesktop.com

Copyright © 2008–2018 Noble Desktop NYC LLC
Publish Date: 01-18-2019

All rights reserved. No part of this book may be reproduced or transmitted in any form by any means, electronic, mechanical, photocopy, recording, or otherwise without express written permission from the publisher. For information on reprint rights, please contact
hello@nobledesktop.com

The publisher makes no representations or warranties with respect to the accuracy or completeness of the contents of this work, and specifically disclaims any warranties. Noble Desktop shall not have any liability to any person or entity with respect to any loss or damage caused or alleged to be caused directly or indirectly by the instructions contained in this book or by the computer software and hardware products described in it. Further, readers should be aware that software updates can make some of the instructions obsolete, and that websites listed in this work may have changed or disappeared since publication.

Adobe, the Adobe Logo, Creative Cloud, and Adobe app names are trademarks of Adobe Systems Incorporated. Apple and macOS are trademarks of Apple Inc. registered in the U.S. and other countries. Microsoft and Windows are either registered trademarks or trademarks of Microsoft Corporation in the U.S. and other countries. All other trademarks are the property of their respective owners.

Table of Contents

SETUP & INTRODUCTION

Downloading the Class Files 7

The Tools Panel Expanded & Keyboard Shortcuts 9

INFO & EXERCISES

SECTION 1

Exercise 1A: InDesign: Letter Creation 11
Topics: Setting preferences
The Control panel
Text frames
Basic text attributes
Basic keyboard shortcuts

Exercise 1B: InDesign: More Text Styling 17
Topics: Baseline shift
Small caps
The Line tool
Making proper fractions

Exercise 1C: InDesign: Advanced Word Processing/Formatting 21
Topics: Paragraph spacing
Tabs

Exercise 1D: InDesign: Kerning/Tracking 25
Topics: Optical vs. metric kerning
Kerning vs. tracking
Manual kerning

Exercise 1E: InDesign: 2-Page Magazine Ad 27
Topics: Facing pages
Color swatches
Defining colors

Exercise 1F: InDesign: Multiple Column Ad with Text Wrap 33
Topics: Multiple text columns
Drop caps
The baseline grid
Text wrap

Table of Contents

Exercise 1G: InDesign: Magazine Cover 41
Topics: Placing transparent art
Defining & using color swatches
Type on a path

Exercise 1H: InDesign: Style Sheets in a Magazine Article 49
Topics: Paragraph styles
Character styles
Nested styles

SECTION 2

Exercise 2A: Photoshop: Getting Started 59
Topics: Zooming
Scrolling
Getting around
Tools
Copying & pasting

Exercise 2B: Photoshop: Photo Retouching 65
Topics: Making selections
The Healing Brush tool
The Clone Stamp tool
The Red Eye tool

Exercise 2C: Photoshop: Replacing Backgrounds 69
Topics: The Magic Wand tool
Image compositing

Exercise 2D: Photoshop: Annual Report Cover 73
Topics: More selection practice
Feathering selections
Working with layers
Using type

Exercise 2E: Photoshop: Selecting with Quick Masks 79
Topics: Quick masks
More Magic Wand tool practice

Exercise 2F: Photoshop: Cropping, Resizing, & Blending 83
Topics: The Gradient tool
More pattern practice
Blending modes

Table of Contents

Exercise 2G: Photoshop: Preparing Digital Photos for Print 89
Topics: Viewing/setting image size
Resampling pros & cons
Saving as PSD
Saving as TIFF

Exercise 2H: Photoshop: Saving Photos for the Web as JPEG 91
Topics: Resizing images for the web
Reducing image size with resampling
Setting JPEG quality

Exercise 2I: Photoshop: Saving Photos for the Web as GIF/PNG 95
Topics: Comparing GIF & PNG
Transparency on the web

Exercise 2J: Photoshop: Adjustment Layers & Masks 99
Topics: More Curves practice
Masking out unwanted adjustments
Organizing layers into groups

Exercise 2K: Photoshop: Using Layer Masks for Silhouettes 105
Topics: The Magnetic Lasso tool
More practice with layer masks
The Refine Edge dialog
Color Fill layers

SECTION 3

Exercise 3A: Illustrator Preferences: Do Before Remaining Exercises! 109
Topics: Setting up preferences & workspaces

Exercise 3B: Illustrator: Straight Lines 111
Topics: Using the Pen tool
Adjusting the workspace
Arranging objects
Color fills

Exercise 3C: Illustrator: Curves 115
Topics: Drawing curves with the Pen tool
Anchor points & direction points
Default fill & stroke

Exercise 3D: Illustrator: Corners & Curves 117
Topics: Drawing corners & curves with the Pen tool
Adjusting anchor points

Table of Contents

Exercise 3E: Illustrator: No Smoking Sign 121
Topics: Fill & stroke
Basic shape tools
Grouping objects
The Layers panel
Working with templates
Saving Illustrator files: options

Exercise 3F: Illustrator: Super Hero 127
Topics: Live Trace & Live Paint
Tracing hand-drawn images
Coloring Live Paint objects
Brushes
The Flare tool

Exercise 3G: Illustrator: Juggling Colors & Gradients 133
Topics: Dashed lines & stroke options
Saving colors as swatches
Blending modes
The Gradient tool
Saving gradient swatches

Exercise 3H: Illustrator: Combining Shapes with the Pathfinder 141
Topics: Merging paths (Pathfinder)
Transparency options
Grouping objects

Topics: Placing text, photos, & illustrations
Gradient swatches
Drop shadows
Alignment
Text wrap

REFERENCE MATERIAL

Noble's Other Workbooks 157

Downloading the Class Files

Thank You for Purchasing a Noble Desktop Course Workbook!

These instructions tell you how to install the class files you'll need to go through the exercises in this workbook.

Downloading & Installing Class Files

1. Navigate to the **Desktop**.

2. Create a **new folder** called **Class Files** (this is where you'll put the files after they have been downloaded).

3. Go to **nobledesktop.com/download**

4. Enter the code **adobe-cc18-1801-16**

5. If you haven't already, click **Start Download**.

6. After the **.zip** file has finished downloading, be sure to unzip the file if it hasn't been done for you. You should end up with a folder that has three folders inside: **Illustrator Class**, **InDesign Class**, and **Photoshop Class**.

7. Drag the downloaded folders into the **Class Files** folder you just made. These are the files you will use while going through the workbook.

8. If you still have the downloaded .zip file, you can delete that. That's it! Enjoy.

The Tools Panel Expanded & Keyboard Shortcuts

We included several PDFs in **Desktop > Class Files** that you can refer to in this class as well as your future Creative Cloud adventures.

The Tools Panel Expanded (Find Hidden Tools)

To save space in each Creative Cloud application's **Tools** panel, Adobe hides some tools behind other tools. Sometimes finding a tool is difficult, so we created reference PDFs for each application. They show all the tools and their keystrokes (if available). Here's where to find the PDF files in the provided class files:

Illustrator: **Illustrator Class > Illustrator CC 2018 Tools Panel Expanded.pdf**
InDesign: **InDesign Class > InDesign CC 2018 Tools Panel Expanded.pdf**
Photoshop: **Photoshop Class > Photoshop CC 2018 Tools Panel Expanded.pdf**

Keyboard Shortcuts

Keyboard shortcuts let you use an application faster. Not all keystrokes are shown in application's menus, so we've created single-page references of the best keystrokes. Here's where to find the PDF files in the provided class files:

Mac

Illustrator: **Illustrator Class > Illustrator CC 2018 Shortcuts Mac.pdf**
InDesign: **InDesign Class > InDesign CC 2018 Shortcuts Mac.pdf**
Photoshop: **Photoshop Class > Photoshop CC 2018 Shortcuts Mac.pdf**

Windows

Illustrator: **Illustrator Class > Illustrator CC 2018 Shortcuts Windows.pdf**
InDesign: **InDesign Class > InDesign CC 2018 Shortcuts Windows.pdf**
Photoshop: **Photoshop Class > Photoshop CC 2018 Shortcuts Windows.pdf**

InDesign: Letter Creation

1A

Exercise Preview

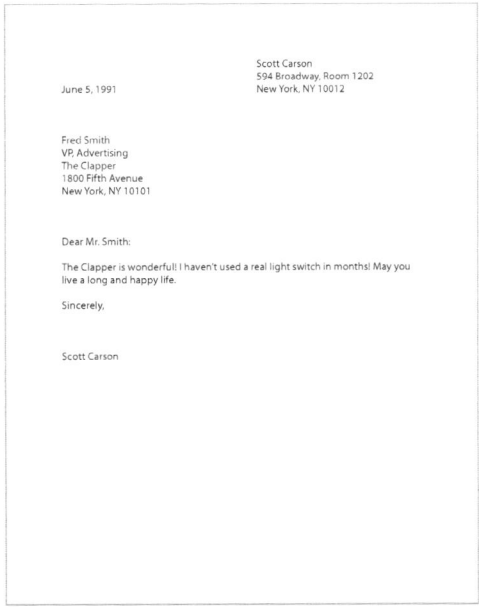

Exercise Overview

A basic letter—this is about as simple as it gets! This exercise will introduce you to the basics of creating a document, drawing text boxes, and formatting text.

Setting InDesign's Default Measurements

1. **Download the class files**. Refer to the **Downloading the Class Files** page at the beginning of the workbook on how to download and install the class files.

2. Launch **InDesign**.

   NOTE: The InDesign exercises in this book have been tested with **InDesign CC 2018**.

3. If you have any documents open, close them all.

   NOTE: By setting preferences before any documents are open, you are setting the default for how new documents from now on will be created. (If a document was open, you'd only be changing **that** document's preferences instead of setting the defaults as we are about to do now.)

4. Go into the **InDesign CC** menu (Mac) or **Edit** menu (Windows) and choose **Preferences > Units & Increments**.

1A InDesign: Letter Creation

5. On the right, both **Horizontal** and **Vertical** Ruler Units should be **Inches**.

   If they are not, change them both to **Inches** now.

   NOTE: Eventually, we will prefer to work in Picas. But for now, all our measurements will be in inches.

6. Click **OK**.

7. InDesign starts with a minimal default workspace that does not show some useful panels. It includes a better workspace though, so go to **Window > Workspace > [Advanced]**.

8. Workspaces remember how they were last set up. To reset any possible changes to your workspace, go to **Window > Workspace > Reset Advanced**.

Creating the Letter

1. From the **File** menu, select **New** then **Document**.

2. Set the following:
   - At the top of the dialog that opens, click on the **Print** tab.
   - Click once on the **Letter** (8.5 x 11 in) preset.
   - On the right, uncheck **Facing Pages**.
   - Expand the **Margins** section if needed.
   - Under **Margins**, make sure the **link** button is checked on, enter **1 in** for any side, then press **Tab** to apply it to all sides.

3. Click **Create**.

4. If you do not see any interface on the left, top, and right of the document (such as the Tools on the left), you are probably stuck in the **Start** workspace (this is a bug). Choose **Window > Workspace > [Advanced]** to show the interface again.

5. Choose the **Type** tool. To place a text frame in the location you want, use the handy arrow that indicates the active part of the type cursor. While it is normally black as shown below, it turns white when you mouse directly over or near a margin or the edge of a page.

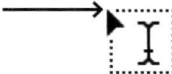

6. Click and drag to create a text frame for the letter, using the margin guides to make sure the text frame fills the whole area inside the guides.

7. The cursor should now be blinking in the text frame. If not, click back into it.

InDesign: Letter Creation

8. From the **File** menu, select **Place**.

9. Navigate to the **Desktop**, then go into the **Class Files** folder, then into the **InDesign Class** folder. Double–click the text file named **LetterText.txt**.

10. From the **View** menu, select **Zoom In**.

11. Scroll so you can see the top right-hand corner of the page.

    HINT: An alternative to using scrollbars is to use the **Hand** tool. To use the Hand tool via a keystroke, hold **Option–Spacebar** (Mac) or **Alt–Spacebar** (Windows). Just be sure to hold **Option/Alt** first, before pressing **Spacebar**.

12. Choose the **Rectangle Frame** tool.

13. Create a small frame in the upper right-hand corner of the page (about **3 in** wide x **2 in** high).

14. Make sure the frame is still selected and from the **File** menu, select **Place**.

15. Double–click **LetterAddress.txt**.

16. With the frame still selected, choose the **Selection** tool.

17. Hold **Shift** and click on the body text frame. Now both frames should be selected.

18. Select the **Type** tool.

19. The **Control** panel that is docked to the top of the screen should be showing the type options shown below. If this panel isn't open, go into **Window > Control**.

    It has two sets of options: **Character** and **Paragraph** Formatting Controls. The two buttons on the left switch between them. If you have a smaller screen, InDesign will only be able to display one section at a time. But if you have a wide enough screen, InDesign will display some of the other section's options in whatever space it has to the right.

    CHARACTER SECTION SELECTED

    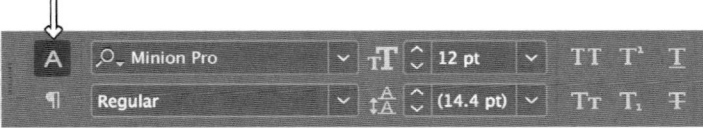

    PARAGRAPH SECTION SELECTED

    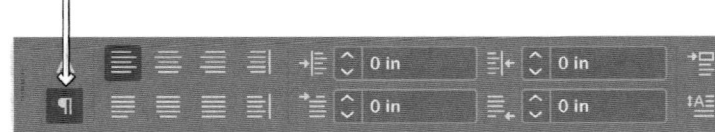

1A InDesign: Letter Creation

20. As shown below, in the **Control** panel, set the following:

    Font: **Myriad Pro Regular**

    Font Size: **14 pt**

Navigating the Document: Zooming & Scrolling

1. Let's get a better feel for moving around within InDesign. We want to see the text larger on-screen. Select the **Zoom** tool.

2. Click a few times on the text. With each click it will appear larger.

3. To zoom out, hold **Option** (Mac) or **Alt** (Windows) and click a few times.

4. Let go of the keys. Let's zoom in a different way. This time click and drag over an area you want to enlarge on the screen. When you let go of the mouse, that area will fill the entire window.

5. Select the **Type** tool.

6. Click on one of the text boxes as though you are ready to edit the text.

7. To scroll around, hold **Option–Spacebar** (Mac) or **Alt–Spacebar** (Windows) and drag anywhere on the document (be sure to hold **Option/Alt** first; see sidebar for details).

   When done, let go of the mouse and the keys.

   > **Scrolling Best Practices**
   >
   > You may notice that sometimes you can scroll by using just **Spacebar** or **Option/Alt**. Since it depends on which tool you're using, we teach you to always use **Option/Alt**, then **Spacebar** so that you don't make unexpected duplicates of objects, or add unwanted space characters to your text.

8. To zoom back out and see the entire page, go to **View > Fit Page in Window** (or press **Command–0(zero)** (Mac) or **Control–0(zero)** (Windows)).

9. Instead of using the **Zoom** tool, we can use keystrokes:

   Mac: **Command–Plus(+)** to zoom in and **Command–Minus(-)** to zoom out

   Windows: **Control–Plus(+)** to zoom in and **Control–Minus(-)** to zoom out

InDesign: Letter Creation

Saving & Printing (Optional)

1. Add a text frame somewhere on the page but outside the main text frame and put your name in it so you'll know which letter is yours if you print.

2. From the **File** menu, select **Save As**.

3. Name it **yourname-Letter1** and before clicking **Save**:

   Mac: If you are already in the **InDesign Class** folder, just click **Save**. If not, navigate to **Desktop > Class Files > InDesign Class** and click **Save**.

   Windows: If the top bar with a file path already says **InDesign Class**, just click **Save**. If not, from that menu choose **Desktop**. Then go into **Class Files > InDesign Class** and click **Save**.

   NOTE: The document will be saved as **yourname-Letter1.indd** because it is an **InD**esign **D**ocument.

4. If you wish, print the letter (**File > Print**).

5. If this was super-easy for you, go to the next exercise: **Large Type Letter**, otherwise finish this exercise.

More Practice

1. Create a second letter. Follow the same steps above to create your boxes. But in the second letter, you will:

   - Place the text **ReturnLetterText.txt** and **ReturnLetterAddress.txt**.

   - Make the font of the text in this letter **14 pt Chaparral Pro Regular**.

2. Create a third letter but this time:

   - Use the text **ThirdLetterText.txt**.

   - Use the same **LetterAddress.txt** from the first letter.

   - Make the font for this letter **Myriad Pro Regular**.

1A InDesign: Letter Creation

> **Creating Text Frames (Which Tool to Use)**
>
> You may wonder why we used the **Rectangle Frame** tool ⊠ instead of the **Type** tool T to create the address' text frame. It's because we already had a text frame under the place where we wanted to create a new text frame. If we had clicked there with the Type tool we'd have started editing the text in the frame that was already there. By making a Rectangular frame first, we don't have to worry about accidentally editing the text underneath.
>
> TIP: How can you tell if you can use the Type tool to create a new text frame? If you see your cursor with a box around it ▸I it means you can create a new text frame. If it's just the I-beam I it means you would be editing the text in the frame underneath the cursor. In which case you will need to use the **Rectangle Frame** tool ⊠ to create a new text frame.

InDesign: More Text Styling

Exercise Preview

Exercise Overview

This exercise gets you pointed in the right direction, showing you strokes, caps, how to make proper fractions, and other professional typesetting techniques.

1. From the **InDesign Class** folder, open the file **uninspirationPoster.indd**.

   If you get a message about modified links, click **Update Links**. The exercise file was created on a different computer and since the images are in the same folder, InDesign will just find and update them for you.

2. We've already typed in the text and done some basic styling such as font and font size. You will perfect the layout. Zoom in on the text so you can see it better.

Styling the "Exploration" Title

1. With the **Type** tool, select the word **exploration**.

2. In the **Control** panel, click the **All Caps** button.

   Don't see it? Switch to the **Character** options via the button on the left.

3. That looks better, but we can make the Exploration title more interesting. Select the middle letters **XPLORATIO** (everything except the **E** and **N**).

4. Make those middle letters (XPLORATIO) smaller, **70 pts**.

1B InDesign: More Text Styling

5. With the middle letters still selected, let's Baseline Shift them to align with the top of the **E** and **N**. The fastest way is to use the following keystrokes:

    Mac: **Option–Shift–Up** or **Down Arrow**
    Windows: **Alt–Shift–Up** or **Down Arrow**

    Try it. Press the keyboard shortcut until the text lines up at the top.

    NOTE: To see how much your Baseline Shift is (or if you don't like keystrokes), look in the **Control** panel. You'll probably need to be viewing the **Character** options A. **Baseline Shift** is near the middle of the panel.

6. To fill out that space we just created, we'll add a line. Select the **Line** tool.

7. Hold **Shift** (to make sure the line is perfectly horizontal) and draw a line that aligns with the bottom of the **E** and **N** and fills in that space.

    NOTE: The line should already be the right color (orange), as we chose that ahead of time for you. If you needed to apply a color yourself, you would open the Swatches panel (**Window > Color > Swatches**) and click on the color to apply it.

8. With the line still selected, in the **Control** panel, make the Stroke weight **3 pt** as shown below:

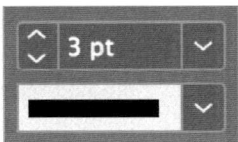

Styling the 2-Line Subtitle

1. Using the **Type** tool, select the two lines of text under **Exploration**.

2. In the **Control** panel, click the **Small Caps** button.

    If you don't see it, switch to the **Character** options A via the button on the left.

The Disclaimer

1. We need to add a footnote number to line 2 of the subtitle. Put the cursor at the end of the second line, after "…**Wrong Way**".

2. Type in a **1** (that's a number one).

3. Select the **1** and in the **Control** panel, click the **Superscript** button.

4. Type another **1** at the beginning of the disclaimer text at the bottom of the page, which starts with "**Not responsible**…"

InDesign: More Text Styling

5. Select it and make it **Superscript** T¹ as well.

   NOTE: Another way of applying options such as **All Caps**, **Superscript**, etc. is by using the **Character** panel (**Type > Character**) and going to its menu. The keystrokes for those options are also shown in this menu.

Making Proper Fractions

1. In the middle of that line is a fraction that isn't properly styled (**99/100**). Select it.

2. On the far right of the **Control** panel, go into the **panel menu** and select **OpenType > Fractions**. (Refer to the sidebar below for an alternative method.)

   > **Proper Fractions Without OpenType**
   >
   > While OpenType fraction styling is ideal, it won't work with TrueType or Postscript fonts. It also won't work with all OpenType fonts! If the menu has square brackets around the [Fractions] option, that particular font lacks the special fraction characters. So one of our instructors, Dan Rodney, wrote a script called **Proper Fraction** that formats fractions regardless of font. You can download a free version on his website at: **danrodney.com/scripts**

3. Since you'll continue to work with this file in a later exercise, be sure to save it as **yourname-uninspirationPoster** into the **InDesign Class** folder.

InDesign: Advanced Word Processing/Formatting

Exercise Preview

Exercise Overview

You will learn the basics of page layout along with more advanced text manipulation. You'll utilize paragraph space before/after, leading, and tabs to complete the layout.

Creating the Letter

1. From the **File** menu, select **New** then **Document**.

    - At the top of the dialog that opens, click on the **Print** tab.

    - Click once on the **Letter** (8.5 x 11 in) preset.

    - On the right, uncheck **Facing Pages**.

    - Expand the **Margins** section if needed, and make all Margins **1 in**.

2. Click **Create**.

3. Go into the **InDesign CC** menu (Mac) or **Edit** menu (Windows) and choose **Preferences > Units & Increments**.

4. Change both **Horizontal** and **Vertical** to **Picas**.

    NOTE: Picas are the default unit of measurement in InDesign, and are often the preferred unit of measurement when styling text.

5. Click **OK**.

1C InDesign: Advanced Word Processing/Formatting

6. Select the **Type** tool and create a text frame that fills the margin guides.

7. With the cursor still in the frame, go to **File > Place**.

8. From the **InDesign Class** folder, select **NewLetterText.txt**.

9. Select the **Rectangle Frame** tool.

10. Create a small frame in the upper right-hand corner of the page within the margin guides (about 2 in x 1 in, or 12p x 6p).

11. Make sure the frame is still selected and go to **File > Place**.

12. Select **NewLetterAddress.txt**.

Formatting the Text

1. In the **View** menu, select **Zoom In** to magnify the text, if necessary.

2. To view the hidden characters, choose **Type > Show Hidden Characters**.

3. Select the **Type** tool (so the **Control** panel is showing type options).

4. With the **address** frame still selected, in the **Control** panel, enter these specs:

   Font: **Minion Pro Regular**
   Size: **13 pt**

5. With the **Selection** tool, select the **body** text frame.

6. Select the **Type** tool, then in the **Control** panel, enter the following specs:

   Font: **Minion Pro Regular**
   Size: **12 pt**
   Leading: **13 pt**

7. With the **Type** tool, click in the 1-line paragraph immediately under the date (**Lenny Bo Benny**).

8. In the **Control** panel (at the top of the screen), on the far left side, click the **Paragraph** Formatting Controls button.

9. In the **Control** panel, go to **Space Before** and enter **2p6** (refer to the screenshot below if you can't find this option).

SPACE BEFORE

10. Click in the 1-line paragraph **Dear Lenny**.

InDesign: Advanced Word Processing/Formatting

1C

11. In the **Control** panel, go to **Space Before** and enter **2p6**.
12. Select the first two large paragraphs of the letter.
13. Make the **Space Before** **0p6**.
14. Select the first line of the table (**Color**, etc.) and make the **Space Before** **0p8**.
15. Select the last paragraph of text (**Well, that's about**) and the paragraph **Sincerely**, and make the **Space Before** **0p6**.
16. Select the last line (**Henny Benny**) and make the **Space Before** **2p6**.

Formatting the Statistics

1. Highlight the entire first line of the statistics (**Color**…).
2. In the **Control** panel, change the font to **Minion Pro Bold**. Don't see this option? Switch to the **Character** options via the button on the left.

   TIP: To choose the bold version of the current font, press **Command–Shift–B** (Mac) or **Control–Shift–B** (Windows).

3. Click in the second line of the statistics (**Blue**…).
4. In the **Control** panel's **Paragraph** options, set **Space Before** to **0p3**.
5. Highlight every line of the statistics including the category (first) line.
6. In the **Control** panel's **Character** options, make the **Leading** **12 pt**.

Tabs

1. With all lines of statistics still highlighted, go to the **Type** menu and choose **Tabs**.
2. At the top left of the **Tabs** panel that appears, click the **Left-Justified Tab** button if it isn't already chosen.
3. As shown below, add a tab by clicking in the light gray area above the tab ruler—the small arrow shows you where it has been placed.

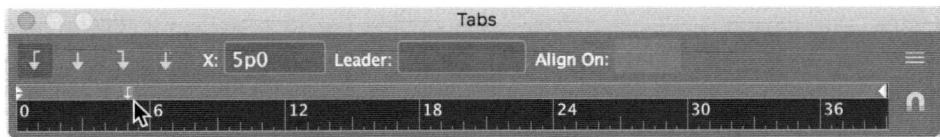

4. Drag the arrow until **10p0** shows up in the **X** field.
5. Click again above the ruler near the **18p** mark.
6. Drag the new arrow until **18p0** shows up in the **X** field.

1C InDesign: Advanced Word Processing/Formatting

7. Add one last tab at **26p0**.

8. If everything looks good, close the **Tabs** panel. If not, adjust the tab arrows ↧ to their proper position, then close the panel.

Wrapping Things Up

1. Make sure the Rulers are visible. If they are not go to **View > Show Rulers**.

2. Choose the **Selection** tool.

3. Click on the body text frame.

4. Grab the **top middle handle** and drag the top of the frame down to about **12p** on the left ruler.

5. Add a text frame somewhere on the page and put your name in it so you'll know which letter is yours if you print.

6. From the **File** menu, select **Save As**.

7. Name the document **yourname-BigLetter**, and then choose where to save the file:

    Mac: If you are already in the **InDesign Class** folder, just click **Save**. If not, navigate to **Desktop > Class Files > InDesign Class** and click **Save**.

    Windows: If the top bar with a file path already says **InDesign Class**, just click **Save**. If not, from that menu choose **Desktop**. Then go into **Class Files > InDesign Class** and click **Save**.

8. Print the letter if you wish.

InDesign: Kerning/Tracking

Exercise Preview

Before — Notice the sloppy, large spacing between the letters, especially between the "O" and the "N".

After — A tighter, more even spacing helps give the heading a polished professional look.

Exercise Overview

Proper kerning and tracking are some of the finer elements of a well-typeset design. Here you will track and kern the headlines to give the title a finished look.

1. Open the file **yourname-uninspirationPoster.indd**. If you didn't get a chance to complete this poster in an earlier exercise, open **uninspirationPoster-Done.indd**.

2. Zoom in a lot on the text so you can see it well.

3. Look at the space between the letters. Look for letters that have gaps between them or are too close together, possibly touching. For instance, the **O** and the **R** in **Exploration** are quite far apart; in the 2-line subtitle, the word **Way** appears two times. There is too much space between the **W** and **a**.

Optical vs. Metric Kerning

Every font has built-in kerning called **metrics**. But not all fonts do a good job of kerning, and what if you have one letter of one font, and another letter of another font? InDesign can do kerning for you based on the shape of the characters. InDesign calls this Optical kerning.

1. Use the **Selection** tool to select the **Exploration** text frame.

2. Switch to the **Type** tool so the **Control** panel displays the text options.

3. Near the middle of the **Control** panel's **Character** options, find the **Kerning** option. From the **Kerning** menu, choose **Optical**. (While it's not quite perfect, it's definitely better.)

4. Use the **Selection** tool to select the 2-line subtitle below.

5. Switch to the **Type** tool and again choose **Optical** kerning.

InDesign: Kerning/Tracking

6. In this case, the kerning is worse! The gap next to each of the W's is now too big. Optical is not always better. It all depends on the font and the particular letters used. Switch back to **Metrics** for this 2-line subtitle.

Manual Kerning

1. Regardless of whether you're using Optical or Metric kerning, you might not be satisfied with the result, so you can manually kern what you don't like. You'll mostly use keystrokes to adjust the amount of kerning, but InDesign's default amount for these shortcuts is a bit big. In the **InDesign CC** menu (Mac) or **Edit** menu (Windows), choose **Preferences** and then **Units & Increments**.

2. Under **Keyboard Increments**, set **Kerning/Tracking** to **5** and click **OK**.

   Note for former Quark users: **5** in InDesign equals **1** in Quark. So a kerning of **1, 2, 3** in Quark is **5, 10, 15** in InDesign.

3. Look through both the 2-line subtitle and the Exploration title for bad kerning. Put the cursor between any two letters and use the following keystrokes to decrease or increase any undesirable spacing. Don't bother with the disclaimer text at the bottom. It's too small for people to really notice.

   To kern in small increments:

       Mac: **Opt–Left Arrow** (decreases space) or **Opt–Right Arrow** (increases space)
   Windows: **Alt–Left Arrow** (decreases space) or **Alt–Right Arrow** (increases space)

   To kern in larger increments:

       Mac: **Cmd–Opt–Left Arrow** (decreases space) or **Cmd–Opt–Right Arrow** (increases space)
   Windows: **Ctrl–Alt–Left Arrow** (decreases space) or **Ctrl–Alt–Right Arrow** (increases space)

   TIP: Remember that **kerning** is meant only to fix bad pairs of letters. If it's an overall, more equal correction you want, then select all the text and **track** it. The same keystrokes work, but **tracking** removes/adds an even amount of space across all the selected letters, whereas kerning adjusts only the space between two letters.

4. When done, you'll probably need to use the **Selection** tool to adjust the width of the rule under Exploration.

5. Save the document as **yourname-uninspirationPoster.indd**.

6. If you wish, print the page, look at kerning, make any adjustments that seem necessary, then print again.

InDesign: 2-Page Magazine Ad

Exercise Preview

Exercise Overview

2-page spreads can be a little tricky to create, but we make it easy for you in this exercise. We'll cover facing pages and page numbering issues to show you how to do it right.

Setting the Document Up as a 2–Page Spread

1. From the **File** menu, choose **New > Document** and set:

    - Set Width to **8 in** and Height to **10.75 in**.
    - Pages: **2**
    - Start #: **2**
    - Check on **Facing Pages** if it isn't already.
    - Expand the **Margins** section if needed, and make all Margins **0 in**.
    - Expand the **Bleed and Slug** section if needed, and make all Bleed options **0.125 in**.

2. Click **Create**.

3. In the **InDesign CC** menu (Mac) or **Edit** menu (Windows), choose **Preferences** and then **Units & Increments**.

1E InDesign: 2-Page Magazine Ad

4. On the right, set the Ruler Units as follows:

   Origin: **Page** (DON'T forget this option!)
   Horizontal: **Picas**
   Vertical: **Picas**

5. Click **OK**.

6. Open the **Pages** panel (**Window > Pages**).

7. The pages should look like a spread as shown below, with a line in the middle that separates the left and right pages. If they are not a spread, you didn't check Facing Pages when creating the document, or you didn't enter 2 as the Start #. To fix it go into **File > Document Setup**, check **Facing Pages**, and enter **2** as the **Start Page #**. Then click **OK**.

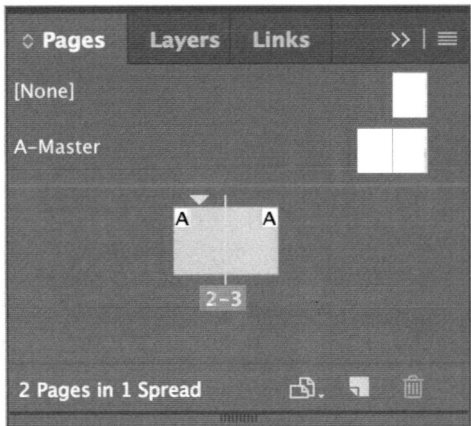

NOTE: The reason this worked is because even numbered pages are always on the left and odd pages on the right.

Bringing in the Picture

1. Go into **File > Place**.

2. From the **InDesign Class** folder, select **time.tif** and click **Open**.

3. The cursor should now be a loaded image icon with a preview of the photo.

   Position the top left of this cursor at the **red bleed guide** (which is **⅛ in** off the top left of the page) and click **once** to place the image.

Making the "Mini" Time Magazine Cover

We are going to put a box around the jeep and put some type in it to make it look like a mini Time magazine cover so your eye is drawn to the action.

InDesign: 2-Page Magazine Ad

1. Choose the **Rectangle** tool.

2. On the right-hand page, draw a box around the jeep that is shaped somewhat like a magazine cover (with the jeep near the bottom). Don't worry about being too exact. Next we'll type in the exact measurements to perfect it.

3. In the **Control** panel, make sure the **top left** reference point is chosen, then enter the four values shown (X/Y and W/H):

   When done, press **Return** (Mac) or **Enter** (Windows) to apply the change.

4. We want to make the frame a specific color, but before we go ahead and create the color, let's make sure the stroke color is active. Open the **Swatches** panel (**Window > Color > Swatches**).

5. As shown below, at the top left of the **Swatches** panel, make sure the **Stroke** swatch is in front (active). If it's not, click it to make it active.

   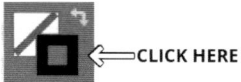

6. Now we can create the color. From the **Swatches** panel menu at the top right, choose **New Color Swatch**.

7. Leave **Name with Color Value** checked and set the following:

   Color Type: **Process**
   Color Mode: **CMYK**
   Color Values: **0% Cyan**, **100% Magenta**, **100% Yellow**, **0% Black**
   Add to CC Library: Uncheck this option if shown

   NOTE: If we did not uncheck **Add to CC Library**, this color would be saved into a shared library available for all documents. We only want to use the color in this document.

8. Click **OK**.

   Although it's hard to see, the stroke is already colored with that swatch!

9. Let's make the line thicker. As shown below, in the **Control** panel, make the Stroke weight **4 pt**.

   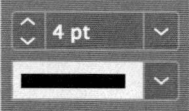

ADOBE CREATIVE CLOUD 2018 • COPYRIGHT NOBLE DESKTOP

1E InDesign: 2-Page Magazine Ad

10. Let's put some type into this box. With the **Type** tool, click in the frame and type in **TIME** (in all caps!).

11. Select that text and make it **44 pt Adobe Caslon Pro Regular**. (NOTE: This font is listed under **C**.)

12. As shown below, at the top left of the **Swatches** panel, make sure the type's **Fill** swatch is in front (active). If it's not, click it to make it active.

CLICK HERE ⇒

13. In the **Swatches** panel, click the red color you just created (it's named **C=0 M=100 Y=100 K=0**). That's how you color type.

14. Before we forget, center the text with the **Align center** button in the **Control** panel.

15. The type is too close to the top of the frame, so go into **Object > Text Frame Options**.

16. Under **Inset Spacing**, uncheck the **link** button so it looks like this:

17. Make the **Inset Spacing, Top: 0p4**

18. Click **OK**.

Setting the Tagline

1. For the type below the image, create a text frame in the white area at the bottom of the **right** page, making sure the frame sits entirely on the right page—no part of the frame should fall onto the left page!

2. Choose the **Selection** tool (make sure the text frame is selected) and enter the following specs. (Be sure to click the **top left** reference point in the **Control** panel):

   X: **2p1**   W: **28p6**
   Y: **52p1** H: **11p8**

3. Using the **Type** tool, type in the following three lines of text:

   If you think watching a volcano in a movie is frightening,
   (press **Shift–Return** (Mac) or **Shift–Enter** (Windows))

   imagine watching one in a rearview mirror.
   (press **Return** (Mac) or **Enter** (Windows))

   The world's most interesting magazine.

InDesign: 2-Page Magazine Ad

4. Select the top two lines of type. Make them **14/20 Minion Pro Regular**. (This specifies **14 pt size** and **20 pt leading**. See the sidebar for an explanation of typographic shorthand.)

> **Typographic Shorthand**
>
> In typography, a common shorthand is to put the font size and leading together.
>
> For example, **9 pt size** type with **12 pt leading** may be written **9/12**.

5. Select the next line. Make it **11/20 Myriad Pro Bold Condensed**.
6. Also set the **Space Before** to **3p** (that's in the Paragraph panel).
7. Go to **File > Save As**, name it **yourname-timeMagazineAd.indd** and save it into the **InDesign Class** folder.

Printing as a Spread

1. Looks like you did it! Well, one last thing. We want to set this up to print as a spread. To do this, go into **File > Print**, but don't click Print till we say! Here you specify a few things:

    - Choose the appropriate printer at the top.
    - Select the option for **Spreads**.
    - On the left, click on the **Setup** section and set:

    Paper Size: **US Letter** (Mac) or **Letter** (Windows)
    Orientation: **Landscape** (the second option)
    Scale To Fit: Select this option

2. Now that everything is set, you can click the **Print** button.

InDesign: Multiple Column Ad with Text Wrap

1F

Exercise Preview

Exercise Overview

This exercise shows you the often misunderstood but immensely important baseline grid. We'll also show you some new text wrap options.

Getting Started

1. Create a new document:

   - Go to the **Print** tab and click once on the **Letter** (8.5 x 11 in) preset.

   - To the right of Width, set **Units** to **Picas**.

   - Uncheck **Facing Pages**.

   - Set **Columns** to **3**.

   - Set **Column Gutter** to **1p6** (or 0.25 in).

   - In the **Margins** section, **unlink** the values and set Margins of Top: **12p11**, Bottom: **18p7**, Left and Right: **4p6**

   - In the **Bleed and Slug** section, make all Bleed options **p9** (or 0.125 in)

1F InDesign: Multiple Column Ad with Text Wrap

2. Click **Create**.

3. Go to **Type > Show Hidden Characters** to view hidden characters.

4. Go to **File > Save As** and name it **yourname-eco-ad.indd**.

Placing the Background Picture

1. Draw a **Rectangle Frame** that fills the **Bleed** guides (red guides outside the borders of your page).

2. Go to **File > Place** and from the **InDesign Class** folder, select **green-grass.tif**.

3. Go to **Object > Fitting > Fill Frame Proportionally**.

4. Use the **Selection** tool and the **content grabber circle** in the center of the image to move the photo up until the tallest blades of grass just reach the bottom of the margin guides.

Importing the Text

1. Make sure the **Rulers** are visible (**View > Show Rulers**).

2. Create a text frame that fills the two right column guides.

3. Switch to the **Selection** tool and keep the frame selected.

4. Go to **Object > Text Frame Options** and under **Columns**, set:

   Number: **2**
   Gutter: **1p6**

5. Click **OK**.

6. Using the margin and column guides, draw another text frame that fills the first column.

7. Into the right frame, place the file **eco.txt**.

8. In the left text box, type **It's Easy Being Green.** (including the period).

9. Select all (**Cmd–A** (Mac) or **Ctrl–A** (Windows)) the text you just typed.

10. Give the text in the left box these attributes:

    Font: **Myriad Pro Bold**
    Size: **66 pt**
    Leading: **54 pt**
    Paragraph Alignment: **Align right**

InDesign: Multiple Column Ad with Text Wrap

11. You will need to make the text box wider to accommodate the text. Extend the left side of the box out past the left margin guide, only enough to fit one word per line.

12. In the layout, highlight the word **Green.** (including the **period**).

13. Open the **Swatches** panel (**Window > Color > Swatches**).

14. At the bottom of the panel, **Option–click** (Mac) or **Alt–click** (Windows) the **New Swatch** icon.

15. Uncheck **Name with Color Value** then set the following:

        Swatch Name: **Orange**
        Color Type: **Process**
        Color Mode: **CMYK**
        Color: **C=0 M=68 Y=85 K=0**
    Add to CC Library: Uncheck this option if shown

16. Click **OK**. You will see that the word Green and the period after it got the new orange color.

17. Give the body text the following attributes (put the cursor in the text and press **Cmd–A** (Mac) or **Ctrl–A** (Windows) to select it all):

        Font: **Myriad Pro Regular**
        Size: **8 pt**
        Leading: **13.5 pt**
        First Line Left Indent: **1p3**
        Color: **[Paper]** (white)

Creating the Drop Cap & Other Type Changes

1. Click anywhere in the first paragraph of the body text.

2. Make sure the **Control** panel is showing the **Paragraph** options and set:

        First Line Left Indent: **0p**
    Drop Cap Num. of Lines: **3**

3. The **R** of the first paragraph looks too close to the text next to it; insert the text cursor just to the right of it (between the **R** and **e**) and kern out until it looks right.

    NOTE: You can kern it out with **Opt–Right Arrow** (Mac) or **Alt–Right Arrow** (Windows), adding **Cmd** (Mac) or **Ctrl** (Windows) if you want to kern out in larger increments.

4. Select the **R** and make it **Orange** (apply the swatch you created earlier).

1F InDesign: Multiple Column Ad with Text Wrap

5. Highlight the line/paragraph **Reduce Your Carbon Footprint**. Remove the First Line Left Indent and make the text:

   Font: **Arial Bold**
   Size: **10.5 pt**
   Leading: **12 pt**
   Color: **[Black]**
   Space Before: **1p1.5**

6. Put a soft return (**Shift–Return** (Mac) or **Shift–Enter** (Windows)) just before the word **Carbon** to bump it to a new line.

7. Highlight the last two words in the last paragraph: **Get Involved.** (including the period) and make them:

   Type style: **Bold**
   Color: **Orange**

Setting the Baseline Grid

Look closely at the alignment of the lines of text in both columns at the bottom of the page. (Zoom in as needed.) They don't line up any more since we changed the leading of the carbon footprint subhead. Let's fix it so both columns align again.

1. In the **InDesign CC** menu (Mac) or **Edit** menu (Windows), go to **Preferences > Grids**.

2. Under **Baseline Grid**, set the following:

   Start: **2p9**
   Relative To: **Top of Page**
   Increment Every: **13.5 pt** (This is the same as the text's leading.)

3. Click **OK**.

4. With the grid set up, we must tell the text to use it. **Select all** the text.

5. Make sure the **Control** panel is showing **Paragraph** options.

6. Click the **Align to baseline grid** button (located to the right of the **Hyphenate** checkbox). The lines in both columns should align again.

7. Click anywhere in the **REDUCE YOUR CARBON FOOTPRINT** paragraph.

8. Click the **Do not align to baseline grid** button.

9. Add a bit more **Space Before** the carbon footprint paragraph so it is now **1p3**.

InDesign: Multiple Column Ad with Text Wrap

Placing the Light Bulb Picture

1. Draw a **Rectangle Frame** in the top-right corner of the page.
2. Switch to the **Selection** tool and keep the frame selected.
3. Click the **top left** reference point in the **Control** panel and set the following:

   X: **41p1** W: **11p8**
   Y: **1p2**   H: **25p2**

4. Go to **File > Place** and select **spiral.tif**.
5. Go to **Object > Fitting > Fit Content Proportionally**.
6. Open the **Text Wrap** panel (**Window > Text Wrap**).
7. At the top of the panel, click the third button **Wrap around object shape**.
8. Set the remaining options as shown:

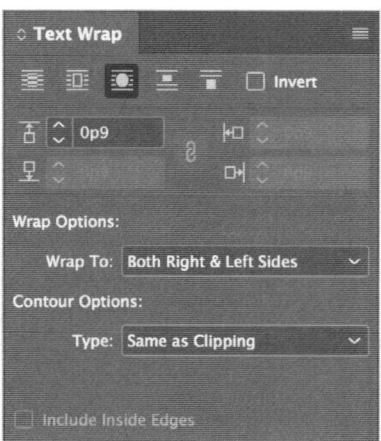

"Massaging" the Text to Fit

We want all of the text to be visible at the bottom of the ad and both columns to be the same length. The last words should be "Get Involved." Notice that the **text overflow** symbol is showing. This means you are missing text. We'll use tracking to squeeze the rest of the text in.

1. To see how much text is missing, select the **Type** tool and click anywhere in the text frame so the blinking cursor is somewhere in the text.
2. Go to the **Info** panel (**Window > Info**). There is a count of the **text you see** plus (+) the **overset text** (text you don't see). It should say something like Words: 350+11 and Paragraphs 6+1. This means there is one extra paragraph of 11 words overflowing. (These numbers may be different for you depending on how much kerning you applied after the Drop Cap R earlier.)

1F InDesign: Multiple Column Ad with Text Wrap

3. Go into the **InDesign CC** menu (Mac) or **Edit** menu (Windows), choose **Preferences > Units & Increments** and set **Kerning/Tracking** to **5**.

4. Select the paragraph right next to the light bulb that starts with **Making homes**…

5. If the paragraph is already six lines, skip to the next step. Otherwise track it in using **Opt–Left Arrow** (Mac) or **Alt–Left Arrow** (Windows). You can do this keystroke up to three times (for a value of –15) but anything more will look bad. This should track the letters in just enough to shorten the paragraph by one line.

6. Select the last paragraph of text by clicking four times in it quickly. Track the text in using the keystroke listed in the previous step until you see the words **Get Involved**.

7. Use the **Selection** tool (while holding **Shift**) to move the left text box up until the top of the letter **s** in the word **It's** aligns with the top of the body text.

Adding the Color Bar

1. Draw a **Rectangle Frame** that fills the width between the left and right **Bleed** guides. Make it **3p3** in height. Its top should meet the top bleed guide.

2. Open the **Swatches** panel (**Window > Color > Swatches**).

3. As shown below, at the top left of the **Swatches** panel, make sure the **Fill** swatch is in front (active). If it's not, click it to make it active.

4. Select the **Orange** swatch.

5. With the rectangle still selected, go to **Object > Arrange > Send Backward**. The color bar should now be behind the light bulb but above the background image.

Adding the Statistic

1. Draw a **text frame** in the top-left corner of the page.

2. Switch to the **Selection** tool and keep the frame selected.

3. Click the **top left** reference point in the **Control** panel and set the following:

   X: **4p6** W: **13p**
   Y: **3p8** H: **7p5**

4. Place the file **stat.txt** in the text box.

InDesign: Multiple Column Ad with Text Wrap

5. Make the text:

    Font: **Arial Bold**
    Size: **12 pt**
    Leading: **15 pt**
    Paragraph Alignment: **Align right**
    Color: **[Paper]** (white)

6. Choose the **Pen** tool.

7. As shown below, draw an arcing **Bézier Curve** from just beside the statistic to the left edge of the light bulb.

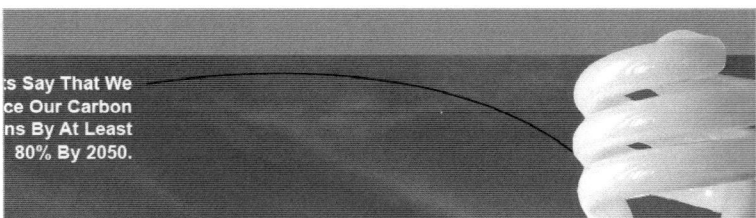

8. Open the **Swatches** panel (**Window > Color > Swatches**).

9. Make sure the **Stroke** swatch is in front. If it's not, click it to make it active.

10. With the stroke still selected, go to the **Swatches** panel menu and choose **New Color Swatch**.

11. Set the following: **C=50 M=0 Y=100 K=0**, and name the new swatch **Green**.

12. Once you click **OK**, the stroke gets the green swatch.

13. Open the **Stroke** panel (**Window > Stroke**) and set the options shown below:

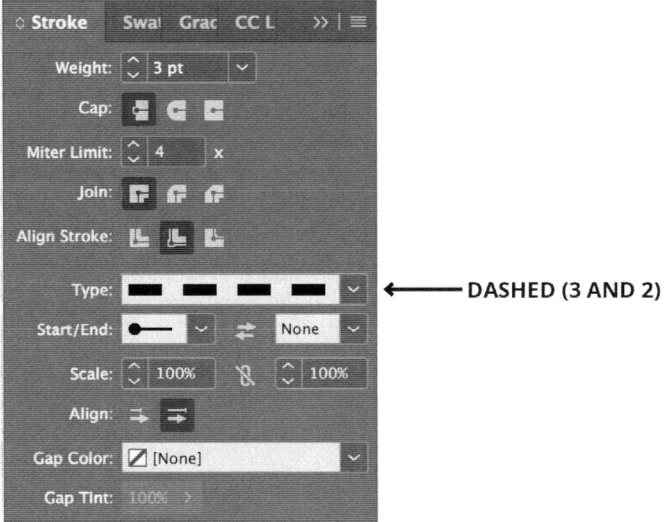

← DASHED (3 AND 2)

14. Make a new text box on the pasteboard outside the page, measuring **W: 7p, H: 8p2**.

InDesign: Multiple Column Ad with Text Wrap

15. Type an **asterisk** (*) and make it:

    - **Myriad Pro Semibold**
    - **130 pt**
    - **Green** (use the swatch you created)

16. Use the **Selection** tool and select the box.

17. Go to **Type > Create Outlines**.

18. Move the asterisk shape to the opposite end of the curve, near the light bulb.

Finishing Up

1. Deselect everything, then press **W** on the keyboard to see the lovely advertisement without guides.

2. Save the document and print if you wish.

InDesign: Magazine Cover 1G

Exercise Preview

Exercise Overview

How did we get the head in front of the logo? In this exercise, we'll show you that trick, as well as the **Type on a Path** tool.

Creating the Document

1. Create a new document:

    - Set Width to **10 in** and Height to **12 in**.

    - Uncheck **Facing Pages** if it isn't already.

    - If the number of **Columns** isn't already **1**, change it now.

    - Expand the **Margins** section if needed, make sure the **link** button is checked on, and make all Margins **0 in**.

    - Expand the **Bleed and Slug** section if needed, and make all Bleed options **1/8 in**.

2. Click **Create**.

1G InDesign: Magazine Cover

Importing the Graphics & Text

We have a couple images and a text file we'd like to import. We can do this all in one shot.

1. Go to **File > Place** (**Cmd–D** (Mac) or **Ctrl–D** (Windows)).

2. Navigate into the **InDesign Class** folder, then into the **Interview Magazine** folder and do NOT click Open until we say!

   - Click once on **charlize.tif** to highlight it.

   - Hold **Shift** and click on **Magazine.txt**. This should also highlight **InterviewLogo.eps**.

   - Click **Open**.

3. A thumbnail image of Charlize should currently be loaded in the cursor. It should have a number (3) since this image and two other files are loaded in the cursor. If the cursor is showing a different thumbnail, use the **Arrow keys** on your keyboard to cycle through the loaded images until Charlize shows up.

   As shown below:

   - Position the cursor at the **top left bleed guide**.

   - Click **once** to place the Charlize image.

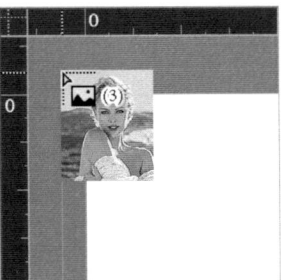

4. The image should fill out the red bleed guides and the cursor should now be loaded with the **Interview logo**.

5. Position the cursor near the top left of the page and click once to place the logo. Do not worry about the exact placement for right now.

6. The cursor should now be loaded with some text. Drag out a text frame to the left of Charlize, on the mountains just below the sky. Refer to the exercise preview as needed.

7. With the text frame still selected, choose the **Type** tool T and make the font **Myriad Pro Bold Condensed**.

InDesign: Magazine Cover

8. To refine the position of everything, choose the **Selection** tool and:

   - Make the text frame start **1p2** from the left of the page and make it about **16p** wide.

   - If needed, move things around until it looks like the sample.

9. Let's center the **Interview** logo. Select it and go to **Window > Object & Layout > Align**.

10. Click the button next to **Align To** and from the menu choose **Align to Page**.

11. Click the **Align horizontal centers** button.

Styling the Type

You will now select various lines of text and set size/leading values. Remember that when we say 14/16, that means **14 pt** Size, **16 pt** Leading!

1. Apply these specs to the appropriate text:

Charlize:	**62/49**
Theron:	**62/49**
She Ain't the:	**24/24**
Girl Next Door:	**24/24**
Photos by Herb Ritts:	**17/19**
Big, Bad:	**35/45**
Brad Pitt:	**46/40**
Pix!:	**79/63**
Why Millions Wish:	**24/24**
He Were the:	**24/24**
Boy Next Door:	**24/24**
Clip 'n' Save!:	**21/21** [Make font **Brush Script Std**]
by Steven Klein:	**17/19**

2. Draw a small text frame under the "**ew**" of the Interview logo. This is for the date of the issue.

3. Type the following into that text frame: **Novembrrrr 2018** (or the current year).

4. Change it to **14 pt Myriad Pro Bold Condensed**.

Coloring the Type

1. Make sure nothing is selected in the document by choosing **Edit > Deselect All**.

1G InDesign: Magazine Cover

2. It's time to create some colors for the text, but first let's get rid of InDesign's default colors that we won't be using. Open the **Swatches** panel.

   We have the standard InDesign colors such as a cyan, magenta, etc., but we also have Pantone 200 CVC. How did that get there? When we imported the Interview logo, it brought with it the spot color Pantone 200 CVC. Wow, what will they think of next?

3. Go into the **Swatches** panel menu and choose **Select All Unused**.

4. Click the **Delete** button at the bottom of the panel.

5. We need to create two colors. Go into the **Swatches** panel menu and choose **New Color Swatch**.

6. With **Add to CC Library** unchecked if shown, set the following but DON'T click OK until we say!

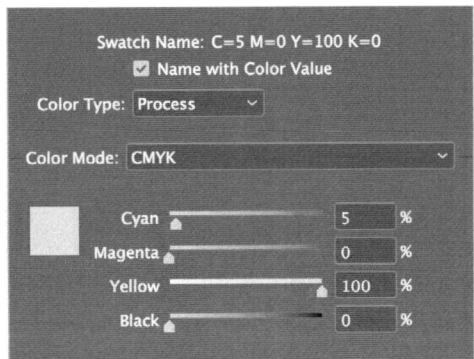

7. Once you've entered the above color, click **Add** once (do not click OK!). This way you are still in the New Color Swatch window and we can make the second color.

8. Mix up the following color:

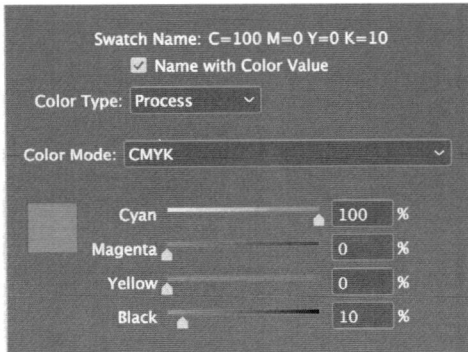

9. Click **OK**.

10. We'll start by making all the text on the left white (the color of the paper we're printing on). Select the text.

InDesign: Magazine Cover

11. As shown below, at the top left of the **Swatches** panel, make sure the type's **Fill** swatch is in front (active). If it's not, click it to make it active.

12. In the **Swatches** panel, click the **[Paper]** swatch to apply it.

13. Now we'll add dollops of color by selecting some text and choosing the appropriate swatch in the **Swatches** panel. Select the text **Charlize Theron**.

14. Click on the **yellow** swatch named (C=5 M=0 Y=100 K=0). The text color might look weird, but it will be yellow when you deselect.

15. Make the following words the same **yellow** swatch:
    - Herb Ritts
    - Big, Bad Brad Pitt Pix!
    - Clip 'n' Save!
    - The "by" on the bottom line

16. See that **Novembrrrr 2018** (or current year) in the upper right of the page? Make that **Pantone 200 CVC**.

17. Select only the **brrrr** and make it the **blue** swatch (named **C=100 M=0 Y=0 K=10**). Lookin' good!

Bringing Charlize's Head in Front of the Logo

Notice that the Interview logo is covering Charlize's head. This is simply unacceptable! We need to bring in another file, in which the background has been removed leaving only Charlize's forehead and hair, so that we can place it in front of the logo without the background showing up. Thankfully, this has already been done in Photoshop, which is the best place to do it. All you must do is import the silhouette and place it just right. It's easy if you follow these steps.

1. With the **Selection** tool, click on the Charlize picture frame to select it.
2. Copy it (**Edit > Copy**).
3. Go to **Edit > Paste in Place**.
4. The type and logo will look like they've disappeared, but don't worry. We've just made a second picture frame in front of everything, so it's only temporarily covering over the type and logo.

1G InDesign: Magazine Cover

5. Now we can replace the Charlize picture by importing a silhouetted Charlize forehead into this latest frame. With the frame still selected, go to **File > Place** and choose **charlize silo.psd**.

   NOTE: Because the forehead frame is now on top of everything, you won't be able to select the text, logo, etc. just by clicking on them. If you need to change the text, hold **Command** (Mac) or **Control** (Windows) and click on it. Wow, you reached right through that top frame! With the text frame selected, go to **Object > Arrange > Bring to Front** so you won't have to keep using the keystroke to select it each time.

The Final Touches

This cover is almost ready. However, let's add the word **Introducing** above the words **Charlize Theron**. In a twist, let's make it flowing type on a path. We'll try to draw a Bézier line riding the mountain range as shown in our example below.

1. Do an **Edit > Deselect All**.

2. Let's make sure we have a stroke color, but no fill. Near the bottom of the **Tools** panel, below the Fill/Stroke swatches, click the **Default Fill and Stroke** button .

3. Select the **Pen** tool .

4. This can be tricky, but we'll do our best. To get the curve we are looking for, you need to create three anchor points, dragging to the right every time, but sometimes up, sometimes down. Below, you see what the path should look like. If you have trouble, ask the instructor for help.

5. Once you have the right path going along the mountain range, select the **Type on a Path** tool . Click and hold on the **Type** tool to choose this tool.

6. Click once on the path you just drew and type in the following text: **Introducing**

7. Make that word **38 pt Brush Script Std** and set its color to **Pantone 200 CVC**.

8. Choose the **Selection** tool .

InDesign: Magazine Cover

9. The stroke (and fill if there is one) must be removed. At the top of the **Swatches** panel:

    - Make sure the **Formatting affects container** button is selected.
    - Make the **Stroke** (or **Fill**) active.
    - Click the **[None]** swatch to remove it.

10. Now that you see the type by itself, you may find you want to adjust the path. Go ahead and do it using the **Direct Selection** tool.

11. If you want, save the file as **yourname-magazineCover**.

12. When happy with everything, you are ready to print (if you want). Since this document is 10 in by 12 in, you need to print on 11x17 size paper or reduce it to fit on Letter (8.5x11) paper. The following instructions describe how to print.

13. If you want, go into **File > Print** and set the following options:

    - Under **Printer**, choose **[the name of your printer]**.
    - On the left, click on the **Marks and Bleed** section.
    - Check **Crop Marks**.
    - Under Bleed and Slug, check **Use Document Bleed Settings**.
    - On the left, click on the **Advanced** section.
    - Under **Transparency Flattener**, choose **[High Resolution]**.

    ### To print on Letter (8.5x11) paper:
    - On the left, click on the **Setup** section.
    - Under **Paper Size**, choose **US Letter** (Mac) or **Letter** (Windows).
    - Under **Scale**, select **Scale To Fit**.

    ### To print on Tabloid (11x17) paper:
    - On the left, click on the **Setup** section.
    - Under **Paper Size**, choose **11x17**.
    - Under **Scale**, leave Width & Height: **100%**. (Don't select Scale To Fit.)

14. Look at the Preview on the left to make sure things look OK, then click **Print**.

InDesign: Style Sheets in a Magazine Article

Exercise Preview

Exercise Overview

Paragraph and character styles are some of the most important tools you have in InDesign. We show you the basics here, as well as the more advanced and powerful nested styles.

1. Open the file **Popcorn.indd**. (If you get a message about modified links, click **Update Links**. The exercise file was created on a different computer, but InDesign will automatically find the files for you in their expected folder.)

2. Do a **File > Save As** and save it as **yourname-Popcorn.indd**.

3. In the **InDesign CC** menu (Mac) or **Edit** menu (Windows), go to **Preferences > Type**.

4. Check on **Apply Leading to Entire Paragraphs** and click **OK**.

Importing the Text

1. Choose the **Selection** tool and select the 4-column text box on the page.

1H InDesign: Style Sheets in a Magazine Article

2. Do a **File > Place**, and choose **pop.txt**. If you get a missing font alert, do the following instructions. Otherwise continue to the next step:

   - Click the **Find Fonts** button (or if you missed clicking it, go into **Type > Find Font**).
   - At the top, select the missing font (which is probably Times in this case).
   - At the bottom of the window, under **Replace With: Font Family**, choose **Times** (or any font you have, it really doesn't matter in this case).
   - Click **Change All**.
   - Click **Done**.

Styling the Band Name

Typically when starting a design, you don't know how you want the text to look, so the first thing you do is style it. Then once you like it, you save that appearance as a style so you can apply it elsewhere.

1. Go into **Type > Show Hidden Characters** to see things like Paragraph markers.
2. Select the first word: **Stereolab** (this is a 1-word paragraph).
3. Make it **14/12.5 Myriad Pro Bold**.
4. We haven't yet defined the color we want. But before we create it, keep the text selected and open the **Swatches** panel (**Window > Color > Swatches**).
5. At the top left of the **Swatches** panel, make sure the type's **Fill** swatch is in front (active). If it's not, click it to make it active.

6. Go into the **Swatches** panel menu and choose **New Color Swatch**.
7. Make sure **Add to CC Library** is unchecked if shown, then enter these settings:

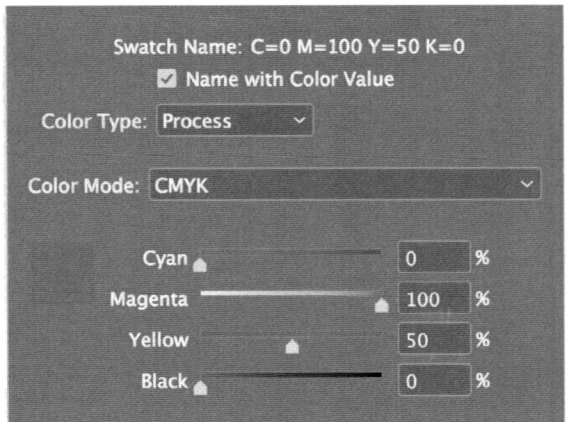

InDesign: Style Sheets in a Magazine Article

8. When done with the color, click **OK**.

9. The "pink" color swatch (named **C=0 M=100 Y=50 K=0**) you just created is added to the bottom of the panel and has been applied for you.

Styling the Regular Text

1. Select the next **two** paragraphs: from **Dots and Loops** through **Lorraine Ali**.

2. Give it the following text attributes:

   Font: **Myriad Pro Regular**
   Size: **9 pt**
   Leading: **12.5 pt**
   Alignment: **Justify with last line aligned left**

3. Go into the **Control** panel menu and choose **Hyphenation**.

4. Enter the following settings:

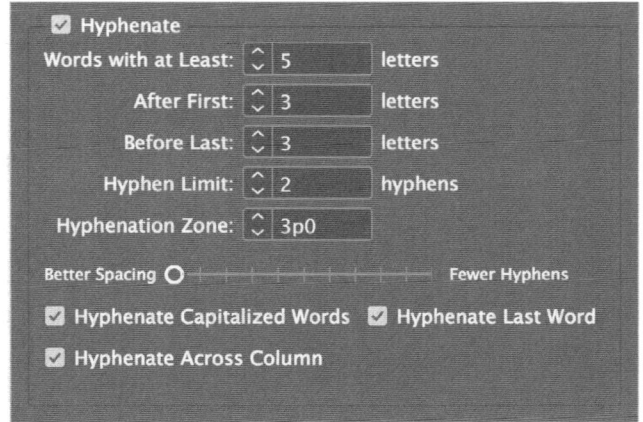

5. When done, click **OK**.

6. Go back into the **Control** panel menu and choose **Justification**.

7. Enter the following settings:

InDesign: Style Sheets in a Magazine Article

8. When done, click **OK**.

9. Select all **three** of the paragraphs you just styled: **Stereolab** through **Lorraine Ali**.

10. In the **Control** panel's **Paragraph** options, click **Align to baseline grid**.

11. Select the second line, **Dots and Loops (Elektra)**.

12. Give it the following attributes:

    Font: **Myriad Pro Italic**
    Alignment: **Left**

Creating Paragraph Styles

We're ready to create the styles. Let's start with the band name.

1. Click anywhere in the first paragraph, **Stereolab** (it's only a 1-word paragraph).

2. Open the **Paragraph Styles** panel (**Type > Paragraph Styles**).

3. Go into the **Paragraph Styles** panel menu and choose **New Paragraph Style**.

4. Name this one **Band Name**.

5. InDesign can also save paragraph styles into a CC Library. We only want to use this style in the current document, so uncheck **Add to CC Library** if the option is shown.

6. Click **OK**.

   NOTE: You didn't have to set anything in the style sheet since InDesign copied all of the settings from the paragraph the cursor was in!

7. Let's create another style for the album info. Click anywhere in the second line. This is a 1-line paragraph that reads: **Dots and Loops (Elektra)**.

8. In the **Paragraph Styles** panel menu, choose **New Paragraph Style**.

9. Name this one **Album Info** and click **OK**.

10. One more style for the regular text—click anywhere in the large paragraph below that. It begins: **Stereolab take their**…

11. In the **Paragraph Styles** panel menu, choose **New Paragraph Style**.

    TIP: A faster way to create a style is to hold **Option** (Mac) or **Alt** (Windows) and click the **New style** button at the bottom of the panel. (If you don't hold **Alt/Option** while clicking the button, InDesign will give the style a generic name.)

12. Name this one **Body** and click **OK**.

InDesign: Style Sheets in a Magazine Article

Applying the Styles

While we have created our styles, none of the text is using them yet. Let's start by applying the **Body** style to all the text.

1. Make sure the cursor is sitting somewhere in the text frame.

2. Go to **Edit > Select All**.

3. In the **Paragraph Styles** panel, click on the **Body** style to apply it.

4. Click anywhere in the first paragraph (**Stereolab**).

5. Click on the **Band Name** style to apply it.

   NOTE: As you just saw, you technically do not have to select the whole paragraph when applying a paragraph style. Paragraph styles will automatically apply to the entire paragraph.

6. Find the next band name (**Photek**) and click anywhere in it.

7. Click on the **Band Name** style to apply it.

8. Continue styling the rest of the **Band Names**. Here are the remaining names in case you can't spot 'em:

   - Tanya Donelly
   - Boyz II Men
   - Helium
   - The Sundays
   - Steve Earle
   - Matraca Berg

9. Under each of the band names is the short (often 1-line) paragraph for the **Album Info**. Apply the **Album Info** style to each of those paragraphs.

Changing Styles Once They've Been Created

It would look better if there were more space between the bands. Let's add some space above the band name. Since we have a style sheet for the band names, we'll just change it and all the band names will be updated.

1. Make sure nothing is selected (**Edit > Deselect All**).

2. In the **Paragraph Styles** panel, double–click **Band Name**.

3. Click on the **Indents and Spacing** section on the left.

4. Set **Space Before** to **1p** and click **OK**.

   All the band names should now have more space before them.

Optical Margin Alignment

1. Before we continue working with our styles, let's improve the alignment of the left/right edges of the columns. Place the text cursor in the text box (or select the text box) and go into **Type > Story**.

2. In the **Story** panel that opens, set the following:
   - Check **Optical Margin Alignment**.
   - Set it to **12 pt** (this setting is typically the same as your type size, or close to it).

   This hangs Roman punctuation like quotes, periods, etc. a bit outside the column so the column "visually" looks better justified.

Creating & Applying a Character Style

1. At the end of each review is the name of the reviewer. Select the first reviewer, **Lorraine Ali**.

2. In the **Control** panel, make it **8 pt** and **All Caps**.

3. Since this text isn't the whole paragraph, it can't be a **paragraph** style; it must be a **character** style. With the text still selected, go to the **Character Styles** panel (**Type > Character Styles**).

4. From the **Character Styles** panel menu, choose **New Character Style**.

5. Don't click OK till we say so! Name this one **Reviewer**.

6. Click in the **Shortcut** field.

7. Hold **Shift** and on your keyboard's number pad (the numbers on the right of the keyboard, NOT at the top), hit **1**. Don't have a number pad? Read the note below.

> **No Number Pad?**
>
> Some keyboards that do not have a separate number pad have one overlaid on the **J**, **K**, **L**, etc. keys. The **Fn** key gives you access to it. Sadly not all do (newer Mac laptops removed the overlaid number pad) so you can't define keystrokes to apply styles without connecting a full keyboard. If you have an overlaid number pad, the keystroke would be **Shift–Fn–J** (which should have a **1** next to it). You must press the keys in that order! **Shift**, then **Fn**, then **J**!

InDesign: Style Sheets in a Magazine Article

8. In the field, you'll see **Shift+Num 1** appear. That means you can use that key combination to quickly apply this style sheet.

9. Uncheck **Add to CC Library** if shown.

10. Click **OK** to close the New Character Style window.

    NOTE: Just like it did before, InDesign looked at the selected text and copied the formatting into the style.

11. With the **Lorraine Ali** text still selected, in the **Character Styles** panel, click on **Reviewer** to apply the style.

    NOTE: The text won't look different but it will be linked to the style now.

12. Go through the text and apply the **Reviewer** style to each reviewer. If you want to do this fast, just select the name, hold **Shift** and press the number **1** on the number keypad. This will apply the style instantly. (If your keyboard does not have a number pad, you will need to click on the **Reviewer** style in the **Character Styles** panel instead.)

    NOTE: If you can't see the last article's reviewer, you can come back to that in a little while once we've fit the text.

Creating a Nested Character Style

1. Look at the second line of text: **Dots and Loops (Elektra)**.

2. The text before the parentheses is the title of the CD. Select just the text **Dots and Loops**.

3. Make it **Myriad Pro Semibold**.

4. Let's turn this into a style sheet so we can apply it to the other CD titles. Since this text isn't the whole paragraph, it can't be a paragraph style; it must be a character style. Make sure the **Dots and Loops** text is still selected.

5. Open the **Character Styles** panel (**Type > Character Styles**).

6. From the **Character Styles** panel menu ≡, choose **New Character Style**.

7. Name this one **CD Title** and click **OK**.

8. Before applying this style, let's look closer. At the start of each **Album Info** line, there's always the CD name (they appear before the labels in parentheses).

   While we could select each one and manually apply the **CD Title** style ourselves, there is an easier way. Because the text always follows a pattern of: **CD Title (label)**, we can have InDesign style the text up to the first parenthesis for us! To do this, we will "nest" the **CD Title** character style into the **Album Info** style that has already been applied to that text. Let's do that now.

1H InDesign: Style Sheets in a Magazine Article

9. Deselect everything by choosing **Edit > Deselect All**.
10. In the **Paragraph Styles** panel, double-click the **Album Info** style.
11. On the left, click on the **Drop Caps and Nested Styles** section.
12. Click the **New Nested Style** button and set the following options:

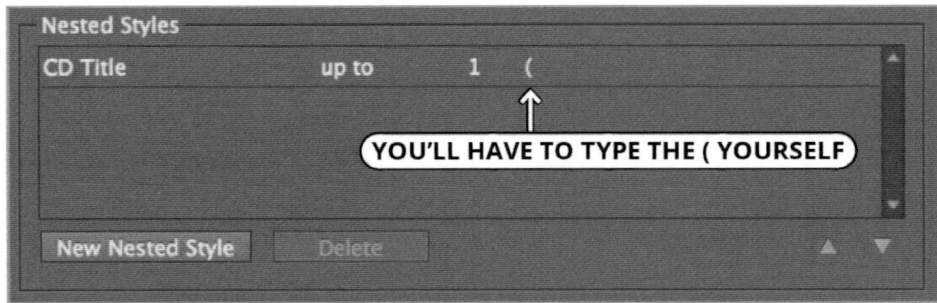

13. Click **OK** and check it out. All the CD Titles are now styled for you!

Adding Space Before Reviewers

1. Notice that all the reviewer names have tabs before them. The reviewer names should align right, so we are going to change these tabs. Here's a nifty way to do it:

   If the name is on the same line as other text:
   - Select the actual tab character (we don't want it anymore so we'll replace it).
   - Then type in a **Shift–Tab** (this is a right aligned tab).

   If the name is on a line by itself:
   - Click to the left of the name and type a **Shift–Tab** (this is a right aligned tab).

2. Repeat the previous step until you've put a **Shift–Tab** before every author except the last one.

   We can't style the last reviewer because the text is not all fitting. Let's fix that.

Fitting the Text

1. Now that we have styled everything, we need to get all the text to fit and then break nicely. We'll be using tracking, and its default keystroke amount is too large. To fix it, go into the **InDesign CC** menu (Mac) or **Edit** menu (Windows), and choose **Preferences > Units & Increments**.

2. Change **Kerning/Tracking** to **5** and click **OK**.

InDesign: Style Sheets in a Magazine Article

3. Look at the end of each review. If the reviewer is on its own line, it probably looks fine, such as with the first three reviews.

   Other reviews such as for the band **Helium**, have awkward breaks. The reviewer **Matt Diehl** has just his last name hanging in the top of the fourth column. To fix this, we'll "cheat" by tracking the text:

   - Select the entire paragraph of the review.

   - Try tracking it in using **Option–Left Arrow** (Mac) or **Alt–Left Arrow** (Windows). (Do not do this more than three times for a total tracking of –15 as more than that will be too noticeable.) That should bring the reviewer's name all onto one line.

   - Try tracking text in or out on other paragraphs as needed to fill the spaces until the bottom of each review looks nicely filled out. If you find a paragraph where too much text spills onto the last line, try tracking only part of the paragraph instead of all of it.

4. That last reviewer, **Henry Cabot Beck**, should now fit at the end of the text frame.

   - Select it.

   - Apply the **Reviewer** character style.

   - Put a **Shift–Tab** in front of it.

   - Apply any tracking you think it needs to look good.

5. Save the file. That's it, you're done! Now these styles can be used for all future issues that use this format for CD reviews.

Photoshop: Getting Started

2A

Exercise Preview

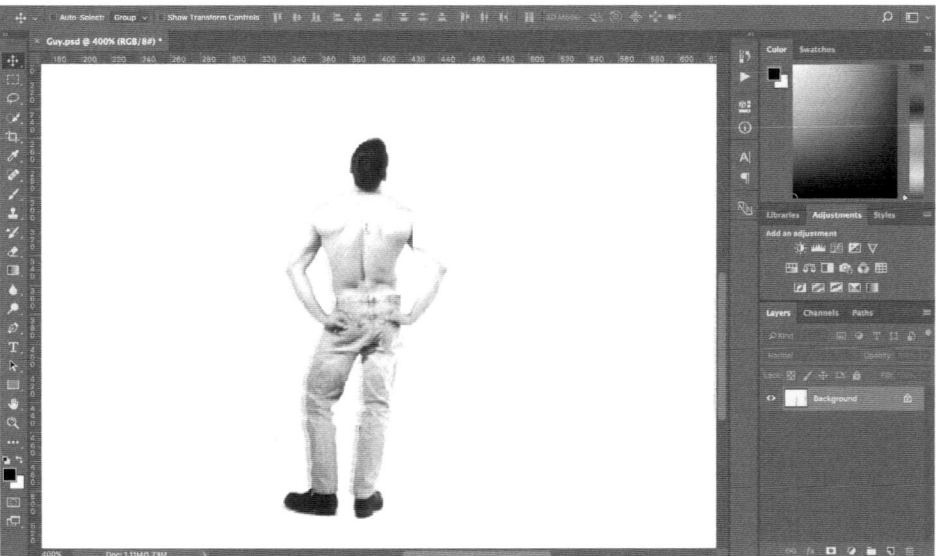

Exercise Overview

In this exercise, you'll start learning the basics of viewing/navigating around images and use some basic Photoshop tools.

Getting Started

1. **Download the class files**. Refer to the **Downloading the Class Files** page at the beginning of the workbook on how to download and install the class files.

2. Launch **Photoshop**.

   NOTE: This book has been tested with **Photoshop CC 2018**.

3. Go to **File > Open**.

4. Navigate to **Desktop > Class Files > Photoshop Class** and double-click on **Guy.psd** to open it.

Restoring Photoshop's Default Settings

1. Let's reset Photoshop's settings, so you have the same settings as this book assumes. Go to **Window > Workspace > Essentials (Default)**.

2. Go to **Window > Workspace > Reset Essentials**.

3. If there is a large **Libraries** panel on the right side of the screen, close it by choosing **Window > Libraries**.

2A Photoshop: Getting Started

4. **Mac users only**: Go into the **Window** menu. If **Application Frame** is not checked, choose it to turn on the application frame.

5. At the top of the screen is the **Options** bar. As shown below, **Ctrl–click** (Mac) or **Right–click** (Windows) on the leftmost tool icon:

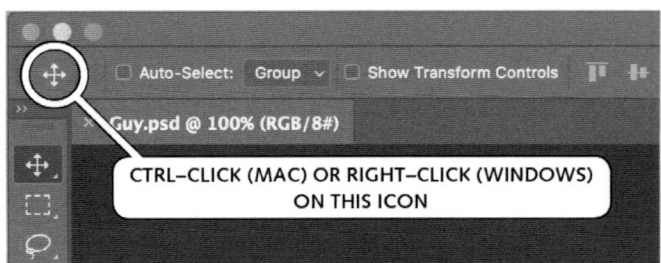

6. From the menu that appears, choose **Reset All Tools**.

7. Click **OK** to confirm.

8. Go into the **Photoshop CC** menu (Mac) or **Edit** menu (Windows) and choose **Preferences > Units & Rulers**.

9. Under **Units**, set the following:
   - Rulers: **Inches**
   - Type: **Points**

10. Click **OK**.

Navigating an Image: Zooming & Scrolling

1. In the **Tools** panel (the toolbox on the left side of the Photoshop window), click on the **Zoom** tool.

2. In the image, position the cursor over the guy's head and click once to zoom in.

3. To zoom back out, hold **Option** (Mac) or **Alt** (Windows) and click once in the image.

4. Let's see a more interactive way to zoom. In the Options bar at the top of the screen, find the **Scrubby Zoom** option.

Photoshop: Getting Started

2A

5. Based on what you see in your Options bar, do the following:

   If Scrubby Zoom Is Checked On

   1. Position the cursor over the guy's head.
   2. **Drag right** to zoom **in**.
   3. **Drag left** to zoom **out**.

   If Scrubby Zoom Is Grayed Out (or Unchecked)

   1. Drag a box over the area you want to see and then release the mouse.

   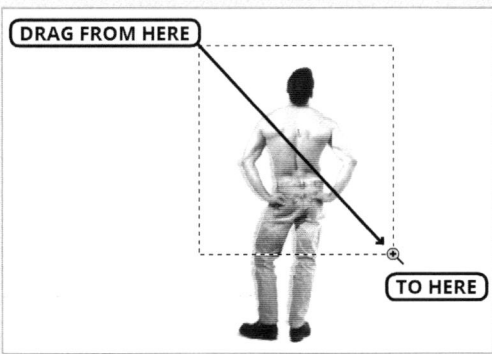

6. To see the whole image again, choose **View > Fit on Screen**.

7. Instead of using the **Zoom** tool, we can also use keystrokes:

   - Zoom **in** by pressing **Cmd–Plus(+)** (Mac) or **Ctrl–Plus(+)** (Windows).
   - Zoom **out** by pressing **Cmd–Minus(-)** (Mac) or **Ctrl–Minus(-)** (Windows).

8. Zoom in a few times so you only see a portion of the image.

9. To scroll around the image, hold the **Spacebar** and drag anywhere on the image. When done, let go of the mouse and the Spacebar.

10. To see the whole image again, choose **View > Fit on Screen**.

Using the Brush Tool

1. In the **Tools** panel, choose the **Brush** tool.

2A Photoshop: Getting Started

2. At the bottom of the **Tools** panel, click on the **Foreground** color swatch:

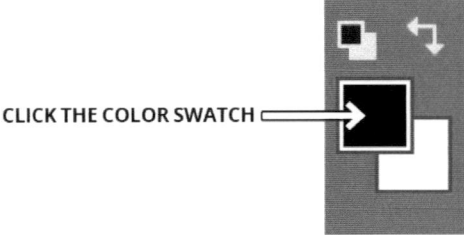

CLICK THE COLOR SWATCH

3. In the window that opens, choose a color as shown below.

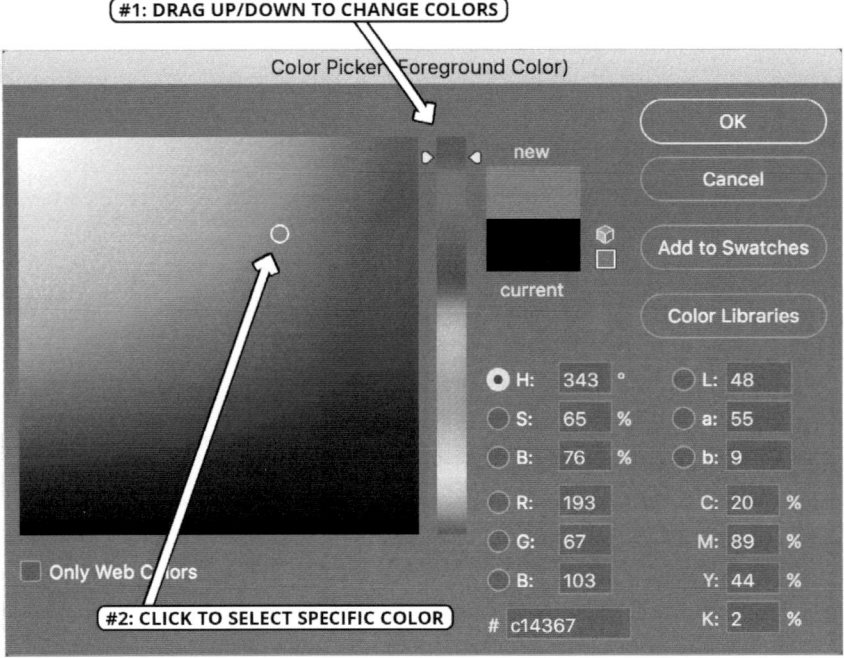

4. Click **OK**.

5. Drag anywhere on the image to paint with the brush.

6. Let's change the brush color. Towards the bottom of the **Tools** panel, click the **Default Colors** icon to set the Foreground color to black and the Background color to white.

CLICK TO SET DEFAULT COLORS

Photoshop: Getting Started

7. Let's change the brush as well. As shown below, in the **Options** bar at the top of the screen, click on the **Brush Preset picker**.

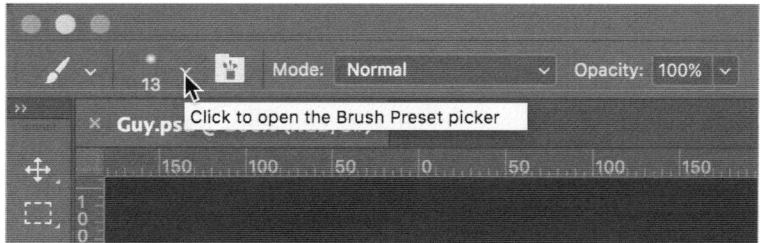

8. Use the sliders to change the **Size** and **Hardness**.

9. Drag anywhere on the image to paint with the new brush.

10. While **Edit > Undo** can undo the very last step, to undo more steps we need to use the **History** panel. Open the **History** panel by going to **Window > History**.

11. Click on the step **before** the **Brush Tool**. This undoes all the brushing.

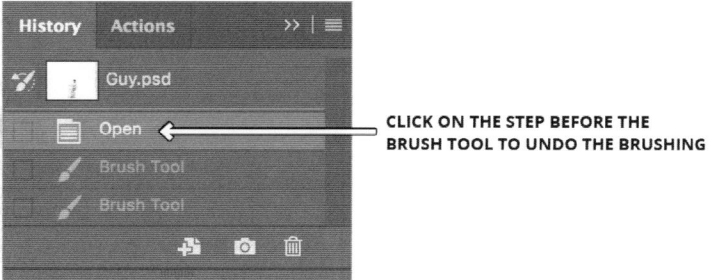

CLICK ON THE STEP BEFORE THE BRUSH TOOL TO UNDO THE BRUSHING

Basic Selections & Copy/Paste

1. In the **Tools** panel on the left, choose the **Rectangular Marquee** tool.

2. In the image, drag a selection box that encompasses the entire guy.

3. Choose the **Move** tool.

4. Drag anywhere inside the selection and move the guy more to the left.

5. Since the guy is already selected, we'd like to make a copy of him. But before we do, on the right of the screen, look in the **Layers** panel to see that there's only a **Background** layer.

6. Do an **Edit > Copy**.

7. Do an **Edit > Paste**.

8. You won't see major changes in the image, but look in the **Layers** panel on the right to see a new layer named **Layer 1**.

9. Drag the guy to move him. Now you'll be able to see that you are moving the copy!

2A Photoshop: Getting Started

10. We don't need this copy, so let's delete it. As shown below, in the **Layers** panel, drag **Layer 1** to the **Trash** button at the bottom right of the panel.

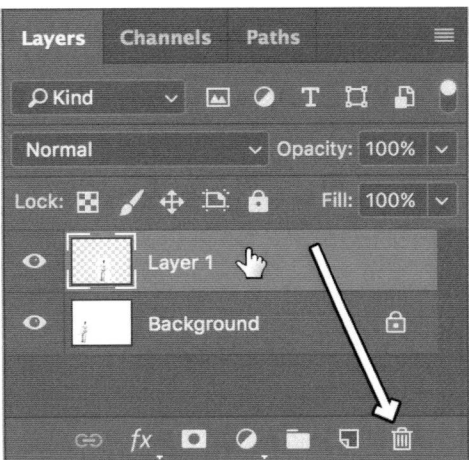

Using the Clone Stamp Tool

Using the Clone Stamp is like copying and pasting, but on the same layer. In later exercises, you'll come to see it's a powerful retouching tool. Let's see how it works.

1. In the **Tools** panel, choose the **Clone Stamp** tool.

2. Position the cursor over the thing you want to copy. In this case, the guy's head.

3. **Option–click** (Mac) or **Alt–click** (Windows) to target it as the source area to be copied.

4. If you're still holding Alt/Option, let go of it now.

5. Move the cursor to the white area to the guy's right, where we want to add the cloned area. Notice the cool preview. It's awesome.

6. **Click and drag** with the mouse to paint. The head you targeted in the last step will be cloned here.

7. That's it for our Photoshop warm up. Close the image without saving changes.

Photoshop: Photo Retouching 2B

Exercise Preview

BEFORE　　　　　　　　　　　　AFTER

Exercise Overview

In this exercise, you'll perform common retouching tasks: eliminating red eye, erasing facial blemishes, and removing an undesired background element.

1. Go to **File > Open**.

2. Navigate to **Desktop > Class Files > Photoshop Class** and double-click on **WaynesWorld.tif** to open it.

Fixing Blemishes

1. We're going to touch up the blemishes in their faces, so zoom in to get a better look. You can do this by choosing the **Zoom** tool and clicking on the image, or by pressing **Cmd–Plus(+)** (Mac) or **Ctrl–Plus(+)** (Windows).

2. Click and hold on the **Spot Healing Brush** tool and choose the **Healing Brush** tool .

3. We need a small, soft brush, so go to the **Options** bar at the top of the screen and click on the **Brush Preset picker**.

4. In the pop-up panel, set Size to **6 px** and Hardness to **60%**.

5. Close the panel when done.

2B Photoshop: Photo Retouching

6. The **Healing Brush** requires two steps:

   - **Option–click** (Mac) or **Alt–click** (Windows) on a good area of the face to set where you are sampling from.

   - Move the cursor over a blemish and click to fix it.

   HINT: Because you are working with skin textures/tones that change over the face, it's a good idea to **Option–click** (Mac) or **Alt–click** (Windows) fairly close to the blemish so that you get the same general texture/tone.

7. Find another blemish on the faces and repeat the process:

   - **Option–click** (Mac) or **Alt–click** (Windows) on a good area without any facial blemishes.

   - Then click on the blemish (or click and drag to affect a broader area).

   Once you've eliminated a few imperfections, move on to the next step.

8. Choose **View > 100%** to see the best representation of the image's quality for print or web.

9. When you are happy with the image, go into **File > Save As**.

   - From the **Format** (Mac) or **Save as type** (Windows) menu, choose **Photoshop**.

   - If you're not already in the **Photoshop Class** folder, navigate into it.

   - Name the file **yourname-WaynesWorld.psd**

   - Click **Save**.

Removing the Hand

1. To remove Wayne's hand, we must completely cover it over with sky. The **Clone Stamp** tool is best suited for this, so choose it now.

   NOTE: You use the **Healing Brush** and **Clone Stamp** exactly the same way, but the Clone Stamp "clones" an area exactly (almost like copying and pasting), whereas the Healing Brush "heals" an area by melding the textures from the source and the tones from the destination (where you paint).

2. In the **Options** bar at the top of the screen, click on the **Brush Preset picker**.

3. Set the Size to **35 px** and Hardness to **0%**. Close the panel when you're done.

4. **Option–click** (Mac) or **Alt–click** (Windows) in the clouds/sky to define the source that you will be copying. Along the right side, you'll want to sample blue sky. Along the left, you will sample the cloud.

Photoshop: Photo Retouching

5. Move the cursor over the hand and click and drag on the hand to clone onto that area. Because the background varies in tone, you'll need to **Option–click** (Mac) or **Alt–click** (Windows) in different parts of the clouds/sky to sample different tones to create something that looks natural.

6. As you near the bottom of the hand, you may have to clone over the top edge of Garth's hair to get rid of all of the hand. Don't worry; you will add more hair later.

7. The edge of your cloud may be a bit even and abrupt compared to the original background clouds. To get a varied edge, go to the **Options** bar at the top of the screen and set the Opacity to **20%**.

8. Also in the **Options** bar, click on the **Brush Preset picker** and select a somewhat small, soft-edged brush. (**13 px** with a Hardness of **0%** should be good.)

9. **Option–click** (Mac) or **Alt–click** (Windows) in the cloud to sample from it.

10. Then click along the edge of the cloud to get a bit more variation.

Fixing the Hair

Now that you have covered the hand with sky, the top of Garth's head probably looks a bit rough. Let's patch up the hair with the **Clone Stamp** tool.

1. Select the **Clone Stamp** and in the **Options** bar:

    - Select a small, soft brush (around **10 px** should work).

    - Set the Opacity to **100%**.

2. Look at the top of Garth's head to determine the overall color and direction of the missing hair. **Option–click** (Mac) or **Alt–click** (Windows) on a section of the remaining hair that matches these characteristics.

3. Click and drag along the top of Garth's head to clone over the missing hair.

4. If it doesn't look quite right, try sampling a different area instead:

    - **Option–click** (Mac) or **Alt–click** (Windows) on the hair you like.

    - Then click and drag on the hair you don't like.

    - You'll probably get the best results by sampling several different areas.

Eliminating Red Eye

Finally, it's time to get rid of Wayne's irritating red eye problem. Luckily we have a tool specifically for this.

1. Choose the **Zoom** tool and zoom in on Wayne's face.

2B Photoshop: Photo Retouching

2. Click and hold on the **Healing Brush** tool and choose the **Red Eye** tool.

   NOTE: If you're using a different workspace, tools may be in different locations.

3. Click once in the red part of Wayne's eye. Voilà! The red eye is gone.

4. Click once on the other eye to fix it.

5. If you want, you can save the file.

   Congratulations—you've completed your first retouching job!

   _____

Photoshop: Replacing Backgrounds

Exercise Preview

Exercise Overview

In this exercise, you will combine two separate photos. The first image features a man against a boring background. To make the composition more interesting, you'll cut him out (often called "silhouetting") and place him in front of the second image.

Using the Magic Wand Tool

1. Go to **File > Open**.

2. From the **Photoshop Class** folder, open the files **baseball.jpg** and **security.tif**.

3. Make sure **security.tif** is the active document.

4. From the **Tools** panel, choose the **Magic Wand** tool. If you don't see it, click and hold on the **Quick Selection** tool and then choose it.

   NOTE: The Magic Wand is a selection tool that recognizes color variations. When you click on an area of the image with the Magic Wand, all adjacent areas of similar color will be selected.

5. In the **Options** bar, set the **Tolerance** to **20**. This makes the Magic Wand select fewer colors, therefore less of the image will be selected. Lower numbers equals fewer colors. Higher numbers equals more colors.

6. Click on part of the green background. You'll find that a large part of it becomes selected but that there are many parts of the background that are not yet selected.

2C Photoshop: Replacing Backgrounds

7. Go to the **Options** bar at the top of the screen. Near the left, you'll find a row of four similar icons. Currently, the first icon, **New selection**, is highlighted. Click on the second icon, **Add to selection**.

8. Click on another section of the green background. The original selection remains and a new selection is added to it.

9. Continue clicking on the green background until all of it is selected. Don't forget the areas between the railings!

    NOTE: If part of the man or the railings becomes selected, just use **Cmd–Z** (Mac) or **Ctrl–Z** (Windows) to undo your most recent step. Then try clicking on a different section of the background with the **Magic Wand** tool. You can also change the Tolerance to a lower number to make the Magic Wand pickier.

10. Choose **Select > Inverse**. Instead of having the background selected, you now have everything **except** the background selected.

11. Use **Cmd–C** (Mac) or **Ctrl–C** (Windows) to copy the selected area.

12. Go into the **Window** menu and choose **baseball.jpg** to make it the active document.

13. Use **Cmd–V** (Mac) or **Ctrl–V** (Windows) to paste the copied image onto this image.

14. Go to the **Layers** panel (**Window > Layers**).

    Notice that the content that you've pasted has been automatically placed onto a new layer named **Layer 1**.

15. Double–click directly on the name **Layer 1** and rename it **security**. Hit **Return** (Mac) or **Enter** (Windows) to apply.

16. From the **Tools** panel, choose the **Move** tool.

17. Drag the security guard down or up to line up his bottom edge with the bottom of the document. You will see pink **Smart guides** when it snaps to the bottom. Release the mouse when you see a Smart guide on both the bottom and right sides.

Cleaning Up

1. You may find that tiny bits of the green background show up at some of the guard's edges. Let's fix this.

2. From the **Tools** panel, choose the **Eraser** tool.

3. In the **Options** bar, choose a fairly small, hard-edged brush. (Try **8 px**.)

4. Use the **Eraser** to carefully brush over the green bits on the edges of the guard's sleeves. (It will help to zoom in for this part.)

    Note that the areas of the security layer that you've erased become transparent.

Photoshop: Replacing Backgrounds

5. When you're satisfied with the results, do a **File > Save As**.

   - Set **Format** (Mac) or **Save as type** (Windows) to **Photoshop**.

   - Name it **yourname-baseball.psd** and hit **Save**.

   - If it asks you if you want to **Maximize Compatibility**, just leave it checked and click **OK**.

   NOTE: Most of the Photoshop class files have been saved as JPEG documents to conserve file size, but you'll always want to save the master copy of your image as a Photoshop Document (.psd). This ensures that the image retains the maximum amount of editability, such as multiple layers. It also maintains the image's quality. JPEG compression reduces the image quality in order to make the file smaller.

   To Maximize or Not to Maximize?

   When saving a Photoshop file (.psd) you may see a dialog with an option to **Maximize Compatibility**. We recommend keeping Maximize Compatibility turned on, so feel free to check on **Don't show again** so you won't be nagged by this option every time you save. If you want to know what this option does, read the following comparison.

   Maximize Compatibility ON
   - The document will be more compatible with older versions of Photoshop.
   - You should maximize compatibility if working with Adobe InDesign.
   - The file size may be larger.

   Maximize Compatibility OFF
   - The document won't be as compatible with older versions of Photoshop.
   - The file size may be smaller.

Photoshop: Annual Report Cover

Exercise Preview

Exercise Overview

This exercise will give you practice making selections, feathering selections, copying from file to file, adding type, and using layer opacity.

1. In Photoshop, close any files you have open.

2. In the **Photoshop Class** folder, open the file **Report Cover.jpg**.

3. To enlarge the image on-screen so it will be easy to do the fine selection work we're about to do, go to **View > Fit on Screen**.

4. As shown below, in the **Layers** panel, click and drag the **Background** layer down to the **New layer** icon at the bottom right. This creates a duplicate layer that we can edit without changing the original image.

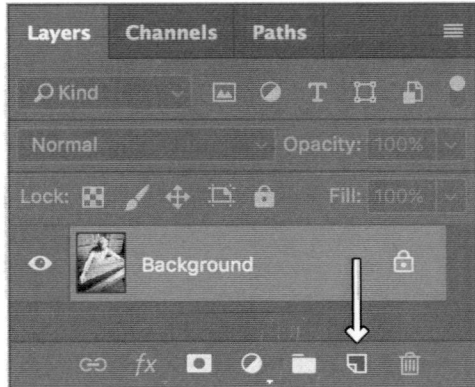

2D Photoshop: Annual Report Cover

Desaturating the Background to Make the Pasta "Pop"

1. Click on the **Polygonal Lasso** tool. If you don't see it, click and hold on the **Lasso** tool and then choose it.

2. Click on a corner of the tray of spaghetti between the man's arms, then move to another corner and click again. Continue clicking on corners until you've returned to your first corner. Click on that corner or hit **Return** (Mac) or **Enter** (Windows) to complete the pasta selection.

3. Once you have the whole tray selected, go into **Select > Modify > Feather**.

4. Set the **Feather Radius** to **2** pixels and click **OK**. This softens the edge of the selection slightly so our adjustment will blend at the edge.

5. Go to the **Select** menu and choose **Inverse**.

6. Go into **Image > Adjustments > Hue/Saturation**.

    - Change the **Saturation** by typing **–75** in its field (that's negative 75!).
    - Change the **Lightness** by typing **25** in its field.

7. Click **OK**.

8. Deselect the selection using **Cmd–D** (Mac) or **Ctrl–D** (Windows).

Adding a Soft Oval Frame

1. If the rulers are not already showing, go into the **View** menu and select **Rulers**.

2. If the rulers aren't in inches, **Ctrl–click** (Mac) or **Right–click** (Windows) in the ruler and choose **Inches** from the menu.

3. Go to **View > 100%**. The rulers should now have a tick mark every 0.125" (1/8"). If it doesn't, you'll probably need to zoom in more (using **Cmd–Plus(+)** (Mac) or **Ctrl–Plus(+)** (Windows)).

4. Go to the **View** menu, and make sure that **Snap** is checked.

5. Select the **Move** tool.

6. Position the mouse over the left ruler. You are going to pull a guide out by clicking and dragging from the ruler. Hold **Shift** (to make the guides snap into place at the tick), then click and drag the mouse so that a guide is positioned **0.375"** inside the left edge. (That's three ruler tick marks from the edge.)

    NOTE: To move a guide after it is set into place, you must use the **Move** tool.

7. Pull another guide down from the top ruler. Position it **0.375"** inside the top edge.

8. Pull out two more guides so that they are **0.375"** from the right and bottom edges.

Photoshop: Annual Report Cover

9. Choose the **Elliptical Marquee** tool (if you don't see it, click and hold on the **Rectangular Marquee** tool, then choose it).

10. Position the mouse at the intersection of the top and left guides.

11. Click and drag to the intersection of the guides at the bottom right of the image to draw an oval selection.

    NOTE: If we hadn't set **Snap**, it would've been much harder to get the ellipse sized and positioned correctly. With **Snap**, it snaps to the guides.

12. In the **Options** bar at the top of the screen, click the **Select and Mask** button. (Prior to CC 2015.5 this was called **Refine Edge**.)

13. In the **Properties** panel on the right:

    • Click on the thumbnail to the right of **View** and double–click **On White**.

    • Set **Opacity** to **100%**.

    • In the **Global Refinements** section, change **Feather** to **15 px**.

    • You should see a preview of this feathered edge on a white background.

    • In the **Output Settings** section, make sure **Output To** is set to **Selection**.

    • Click **OK**.

14. The selection now appears as a line of "marching ants," as they are often called. Even though it may not look like it, don't worry; the selection is still feathered.

15. From the **Select** menu, choose **Inverse**.

16. If it isn't already showing, open the **Layers** panel (**Window > Layers**).

17. To fill the oval frame, we'll use a fill layer because its color can later be easily changed. As shown below, at the bottom of the **Layers** panel, click the **Create new fill or adjustment layer** button and from the menu, choose **Solid Color**.

2D Photoshop: Annual Report Cover

18. In the Color Picker that appears, choose **white** and click **OK**.

19. Double–click directly on the layer's name and rename it **Oval Frame**. Hit **Return** (Mac) or **Enter** (Windows) to apply.

20. Hide the guides from view by choosing **View > Show > Guides**.

Adding the Pepper Picture

1. From the **Photoshop Class** folder, open the **Red Pepper.psd** file.

2. Choose the **Move** tool.

3. In the **Layers** panel, double–click directly on the name **Background**. Rename it **Pepper** and hit **Return** (Mac) or **Enter** (Windows).

4. To copy the peppers into the Report Cover file, do the following:

   - With the Pepper layer still selected, do an **Edit > Copy**. If Copy is grayed out, refer to the sidebar below.
   - Switch back to the design file **Report Cover.jpg** using the tab at the top.
   - Go to **Edit > Paste**.

   > **In Photoshop CC 2017 & Older**
   >
   > CC 2018 made moving layers between files as easy as copy and paste. Previously it was a bit less intuitive. Here's how we used to do it:
   >
   > 1. Make sure both files are open (the file that contains the layer you want to copy and the file you want to put it in).
   >
   > 2. In the **Layers** panel, **Ctrl–click** (Mac) or **Right–click** (Windows) on the name of the layer you want to move/copy and choose **Duplicate Layers** from the menu that appears.
   >
   > 3. Set the Destination **Document** to the file you want to move the layer into. (Next to **As**, change the layer name if desired.)
   >
   > 4. Click **OK**.

5. Look in the **Layers** panel and notice that a new layer named **Pepper** has been created.

6. Use the **Move** tool to bring the image to the lower-right corner. It should snap into place and you should see the pink Smart guides when you get close. Otherwise, you can use the Arrow keys to fine-tune the placement.

Photoshop: Annual Report Cover

7. The pepper image would stand out better if it had a thin black line around it. At the bottom of the **Layers** panel, click the **Add a layer style** button *fx* and from the menu, choose **Stroke**.

8. Set the following options:

    Size: **2 px**
    Position: **Inside**
    Blend Mode: **Normal**
    Opacity: **100%**
    Overprint: Make sure it is **unchecked**
    Fill Type: **Color**
    Color: Click on the color swatch next to **Color**. In the Color Picker that appears, choose **black** in the bottom-right corner.

9. When done, click **OK**.

Adding the Type

1. Choose the **Horizontal Type** tool *T*.

2. In the **Options** bar at the top of the screen, click the **Color** swatch.

CLICK HERE

3. Move the dialog that appears so you can see the red pepper. Mouse over the pepper and notice that the cursor turns into the **Eyedropper** tool. Click with the **Eyedropper** to sample the red from the pepper.

4. Click **OK**.

5. You will be back in the **Horizontal Type** tool *T*. Position the cursor somewhere near the top left-hand corner, then click.

6. Type in the words **Annual Report**.

7. Highlight the text and in the **Options** bar at the top of the screen, set:

    Font: **Times Bold** (or something similar)
    Font Size: **20 pt** (Type in the number.)
    Anti-Aliasing: **Crisp**

8. In order to track out the letters, you must open the **Character** panel. You can choose **Window > Character** or click the **Panels** button on the right of the **Options** bar.

9. Set the **Tracking** to **140**.

Photoshop: Annual Report Cover

10. When done with the type, click the **checkbox** ✓ toward the right side of the **Options** bar. (If it's not there, don't worry—Photoshop already automatically applied the changes for you.)

11. In the **Layers** panel, you should now see a layer named **Annual Report**. This layer has a **T** thumbnail image T to indicate that it is a type layer.

12. Select the **Move** tool and move the type so it starts about ¼" from the top and about ⅛" from the left.

13. Choose the **Horizontal Type** tool T again.

14. Click in the center of the image and type **2018** (or the current year).

15. Highlight the text and make it:

    Font: **Times Italic** (or something similar)
    Font Size: **120 pt**

16. In the **Character** panel (**Window > Character**):

    - Click the swatch next to **Color** and in the window that appears, choose **black** then click **OK**.
    - Set the **Tracking** to **0**.

17. Using the **Move** tool, position the type so it's nicely centered on the image.

18. Notice that in the **Layers** panel, a new type layer named **2018** (or the current year) is highlighted. Above the layer name, near the top of the panel, is the **Opacity** of that layer. Change it to **40%**.

19. Do a **File > Save As**.

20. Set **Format** (Mac) or **Save as type** (Windows) to **Photoshop**.

21. Name the file **yourname-Report Cover.psd** and click **Save**.

    NOTE: Saving as a Photoshop document (.psd) file will save all layers and editable items like type.

Photoshop: Selecting with Quick Masks

Exercise Preview

Exercise Overview

Often, selecting part of an image proves too intricate for conventional selection tools. Quick Mask Mode allows you to use painting tools to create or refine selections, allowing for greater precision.

Starting the Selection Using Traditional Selection Tools

1. From the **Photoshop Class** folder, open the file **watchingSailboat.tif**.

2. Choose the **Magic Wand** tool.

3. In the **Options** bar:

   - Set the **Tolerance** to **32** (this is the Magic Wand's default setting).

   - Click **Add to selection**.

4. Click on part of the water and trees around the man and girl.

5. Continue clicking on the area around the man and girl until most of it is selected.

   - Focus on getting the best selection you can around the man and girl. But don't worry if it's not perfect—we'll be finishing it in the following steps.

   - It's OK if you miss a few spots in the background. That's easy to fix later.

2E Photoshop: Selecting with Quick Masks

6. Go to **Select > Inverse** so the people are selected rather than the surrounding area.

Refining the Selection in Quick Mask Mode

1. As shown, in the **Tools** panel, there's an **Edit in Quick Mask Mode** button.

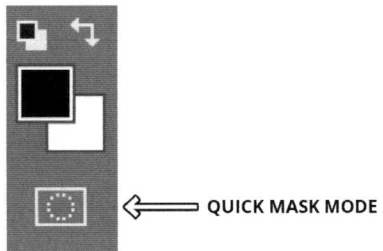
⇐ QUICK MASK MODE

2. Double–click the **Quick Mask Mode** button to set its display options.

3. In the dialog that opens, choose Color Indicates: **Selected Areas** and click **OK**.

    NOTE: You're now in Quick Mask Mode, where your selection is indicated by colored shading instead of the marching ants dotted outline. In this mode, we can change the selection by painting with **black** to **select** and painting with **white** to **deselect**. You won't see black and white as you paint, though. Painting with **black** should appear as **red** unless the color was changed in the Quick Mask Options dialog you were just in. Painting with **white** would remove the color, indicating the area will be **deselected**.

    We want to **add** to our selection, so we need to be painting with **black**.

4. As shown below, in the **Tools** panel, click the **Default Colors** icon to make sure the **Foreground** color is pure **black**.

CLICK TO SET DEFAULT COLORS

5. Choose the **Brush** tool and in the **Options** bar:

    - Pick a **large**, **hard-edged** brush.
    - Set the Opacity and Flow to **100%**.

6. Most of the man and girl are shaded already, but you may have missed some pieces:

    - Completely shade in the large solid areas of the man and girl. We'll get to the edge details in a few steps.
    - Don't worry about the background for now.

    NOTE: You're painting with **black**, which adds shading, therefore **selecting** them.

7. Press the **X** key on your keyboard to swap the **Foreground** and **Background** colors.

Photoshop: Selecting with Quick Masks

8. You're now painting with **white**, which removes shading, therefore **deselecting**. Paint over any areas of the background to remove the colored shading.

9. Check the other edges of the man and the girl. Where necessary:

    - Paint with **white** to **deselect** (remove the shading).

    - Paint with **black** to **select** (add shading).

    - Soft brushes may work better for hair edges, but you'll probably want hard brushes for everything else.

    - To create a feathered look for the wispy hair, you may want to reduce the opacity of your brush in the **Options** bar.

10. You should now be finished painting the selection. In the **Tools** panel, click the **Edit in Standard Mode** button shown below.

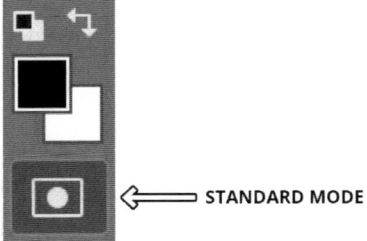

11. Notice that the shading became a selection. Neat!

12. Double-check the selection for little spots you may have missed (the "marching ants" at selection edges should make it obvious). If you've missed an area, go back into **Quick Mask Mode** to correct it, then return to **Standard Mode**.

    NOTE: Quick Mask Mode is only for making selections and will not allow you to edit the image at all. Always return to **Standard Mode** when you've finished making a selection in **Quick Mask Mode**.

Putting the People onto a New Background

1. Go to **Select > Modify > Contract**.

2. Enter a value of **1** and click **OK**.

    By using Contract, we moved the edges of our selection in by one pixel, cleaning up our selection a bit.

3. Use **Cmd–C** (Mac) or **Ctrl–C** (Windows) to copy the selected area.

4. Go to **File > Open**, and from the **Photoshop Class** folder, open **shore.tif**.

5. Use **Cmd–V** (Mac) or **Ctrl–V** (Windows) to paste the copied image onto this image.

Photoshop: Selecting with Quick Masks

6. Use the **Move** tool to position them in the new picture.

    This looks a little awkward since the light on the people is from the left, but the light on the landscape is from the right.

7. Go to **Edit > Transform > Flip Horizontal**.

8. Reposition them on the left of the image as needed.

    Much better! Now the light sources match fairly well and the people have a crisp, precise silhouette, thanks to Quick Mask Mode!

9. If you like, save the file as **yourname-watching the shore.psd**

Photoshop: Cropping, Resizing, & Blending 2F

Exercise Preview

Exercise Overview

This exercise shows you the Gradient tool and how to apply fills with special blending options such as "Multiply." It also reviews selections and patterns.

Cleaning Up the Background

1. From the **Photoshop Class** folder, open **Riddick Bowe.tif**.

2. Select the **Crop** tool.

3. Notice how the whole image is selected, with handles in all four corners and on all four sides. Simply drag the handle on the right to crop out the **BUDW sign**. You can also click and drag in the middle to move the whole cropping area.

4. Once the crop is placed correctly, do any **one** of the following:

    • Click the **checkbox** at the right in the **Options** bar.

    • Hit **Return** (Mac) or **Enter** (Windows).

    • Double–click inside the cropped area.

5. The tone of the black background around Riddick currently varies slightly, and it's not a truly solid black. Select the **Magic Wand** tool so we can change that.

2F Photoshop: Cropping, Resizing, & Blending

6. In the **Options** bar, set the tolerance to **20** and make sure **Contiguous** is checked.

7. Click on the **black** background around Riddick. Let's fill it with a solid color.

8. **Shift–click** on any areas of black background that were not selected to add them to the selection. Don't forget to click between the ropes!

9. If some of the selection cuts into Riddick's body you can do **one** of the following:

    A. Subtract it using the **Lasso** tool while holding the **Option** key (Mac) or the **Alt** key (Windows).

    B. Switch into **Quick Mask Mode**:

    - Double–click the **Quick Mask Mode** button and make sure Color Indicates: **Selected Areas**. Click **OK**.

    - Use the **Brush** tool to paint **white** over any shaded areas of Riddick's body.

    - When done with the selection, switch back to **Standard Mode**.

10. With the selection complete, select the **Eyedropper** tool.

11. To sample some of the dark background color near Riddick's head, click once on the image.

12. To fill the selected area with the sampled foreground color, you can either:

    - Go into **Edit > Fill** and for **Contents**, choose **Foreground Color**. Then click **OK**.

    - Or just hit **Option–Delete** (Mac) or **Alt–Delete** (Windows).

13. To deselect, press **Cmd–D** (Mac) or **Ctrl–D** (Windows).

Adding More Blank Area to the Right Side

1. Go to **Image > Canvas Size** and set the following:

    Width: Set the measurement to **Percent**, and enter **200**
    Height: Leave as is
    Canvas extension color: **Foreground**
    Anchor: Click the **left-middle** arrow as shown below.

    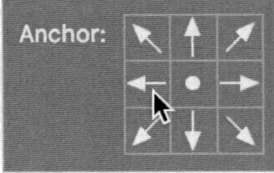

2. Click **OK**.

Photoshop: Cropping, Resizing, & Blending 2F

Making the Ropes Fade Out

1. We want to fade the ropes to the right of Riddick's left leg to black. We'll do this with a gradient, but first we want to create a new layer for it, so go ahead and click the **Create a new layer** button at the bottom of the Layers panel.

2. Double–click on the new layer's name and type in **rope fade**.

3. Choose the **Gradient** tool (you may need to click and hold on the **Paint Bucket** tool to find it).

4. At the left of the **Options** bar, find the gradient preview. As shown below, click the arrow to its right.

5. Double–click the **second** thumbnail on the left in the top row, which is the **Foreground to Transparent** gradient. (If you pause a moment over the thumbnail, the name will appear.)

6. Also in the **Options** bar, choose:
   - **Linear Gradient**
   - Mode: **Normal**
   - Opacity: **100%**
   - **Dither** and **Transparency** should be checked.

7. With the **Gradient** tool, click and drag from the right edge of the ropes to the left edge (stop before you reach Riddick's shorts), along the angle of the ropes.

Creating a Custom Pattern for His Shorts

Now let's make a pattern to place on Riddick's shorts.

1. Go to the **Layers** panel and click on the **Background** layer to select it.

2. Using the **Rectangular Marquee** tool, draw a marquee around both gloves.

3. Copy the gloves (**Cmd–C** (Mac) or **Ctrl–C** (Windows)).

4. Go to **File > New**.

5. In the new dialog under Background Contents, choose **Transparent**, then click **Create**.

6. Paste the selection (**Cmd–V** (Mac) or **Ctrl–V** (Windows)).

2F Photoshop: Cropping, Resizing, & Blending

7. In the **Tools** panel, click and hold on the **Magic Wand** tool and then select the **Quick Selection** tool.

8. The Quick Selection tool will work like the Magic Wand but allows you to paint a selection by clicking and dragging. In the **Options** bar at the top of the screen, pick a medium-sized (about **25 px**), hard-edged brush.

9. To select the glove, start in the center of the right glove and click and drag. Keep dragging around until the entire glove is selected.

10. If you've accidentally selected anything additional, hold **Option** (Mac) or **Alt** (Windows) and click and drag on the parts you want to deselect.

11. Click and drag inside the left glove to select it too.

12. In the **Tools** panel, click the **Default Colors** icon to make sure the Foreground color is pure black and the Background color is pure white.

13. To clean up the selection we'll use Quick Mask Mode. At the bottom of the **Tools** panel, double–click the **Quick Mask Mode** button.

14. In the dialog that appears:

    - Make sure Color Indicates: **Selected Areas**.

    - Under **Color**, make sure the swatch is a bright color like red or green. If not, click on the swatch and choose a bright color that will stand out against the image.

15. Click **OK** to close the Quick Mask Options.

16. Use the **Brush** tool to paint **black** over any missed areas of the gloves you want selected, and press **X** to switch to **white** and paint over to deselect any areas.

17. When done with the selection, click **Edit in Standard Mode**.

18. Go to **Select > Inverse**.

19. Press **Delete** (Mac) or **Backspace** (Windows).

20. Press **Cmd–D** (Mac) or **Ctrl–D** (Windows) to deselect.

21. Go to **Edit > Free Transform**.

22. The Scale options now appear in the **Options** bar at the top of the screen. In the Scale area, between the Width and Height values, click the **Maintain aspect ratio** button to keep it from distorting the image.

23. For Width, enter a value of **20%**. Then click the **checkbox** at the right of the Options bar (or press **Return** (Mac) or **Enter** (Windows)).

24. With the **Rectangular Marquee** tool, draw a box around the gloves that is a little bigger than the gloves.

25. Go to **Edit > Define Pattern**.

Photoshop: Cropping, Resizing, & Blending

26. Name it **yourname-boxing gloves** and click **OK**.

27. We'll leave this file open just in case we need it later, but now switch back to the **Riddick Bowe** file. If you can't see it, go into the **Window** menu and at the bottom, choose **Riddick Bowe**.

Filling the Shorts with a Pattern

Riddick's shorts are a little boring, so let's add that boxing glove pattern.

1. In the **Layers** panel, make sure the **Background** layer is still selected.

2. Click and hold on the **Quick Selection** tool and select the **Magic Wand** tool. Set the Tolerance to **50**.

3. Click somewhere on the light part of Riddick's shorts.

4. **Shift–click** on a few other light areas of the shorts to add them to the selection. Ignore the darker wrinkles for now.

5. In the **Tools** panel, click the **Edit in Quick Mask Mode** button.

6. Choose the **Brush** tool.

7. In the **Options** bar, set the **Opacity** and **Flow** to **100%**.

8. Pick a medium-sized, hard-edged brush.

9. You'll want shading across the entire surface of Riddick's shorts, so use **black** to add shading over the missing wrinkles, sections of the waistband, and any other missing areas. Paint over the words on the trunks, too.

10. If areas outside the shorts (such as the ropes) are selected, type **X** on the keyboard to swap the Foreground and Background colors. Now paint **white** over any shaded areas outside those shorts.

11. In the **Tools** panel, click the **Edit in Standard Mode** button.

12. In the **Layers** panel, click the **New fill or adjustment layer** button and choose **Pattern**.

13. Your boxing gloves pattern should already be selected, so click **OK**. If it wasn't selected, click the pattern thumbnail and choose it.

14. The shorts look very flat right now, but Blending Modes can change the way in which the pattern blends with the shorts. At the top of the **Layers** panel, change the Mode from **Normal** to **Multiply**.

    With the **Multiply** blending mode, this layer can only darken the image behind it, so the dark areas of the shorts on the background layer show through. Feel free to experiment with other blending modes to compare the results.

2F Photoshop: Cropping, Resizing, & Blending

15. The gloves are still a little bright. At the top of the **Layers** panel, next to the Blend Mode, change the **Opacity** to **60%**.

16. If you decide you'd like to reposition the pattern within the shorts, go to the **Layers** panel and **double–click** the layer's thumbnail.

    With the **Pattern Fill** dialog box open, click and drag on the main image to move the pattern. Click **OK** when you're done.

17. Congratulations—Riddick would be proud! Save this as a Photoshop document if you wish.

Photoshop: Preparing Digital Photos for Print

Exercise Overview

A standard print image is CMYK and has a resolution of 300 ppi (pixels per inch). Digital camera images are RGB and often come in as 72 ppi or higher. We will modify an image taken with a digital camera and properly prepare it for print.

1. From the **Photoshop Class** folder, open the file **koala.jpg**.

2. Go to **Image > Mode > CMYK Color**. If you get a message, click **OK**.

3. Go to **Image > Image Size**. Do NOT click OK until we say!

4. Notice that the **Resolution** for this file is **72** but the **Document Size** is **32.444** by **48.667** inches. This means you'd get a large print, but low quality.

5. At the bottom, uncheck **Resample**.

6. For Resolution, type **300**. You'll see that the **Document Size** reduces to **7.787** by **11.68** inches. This means you'd get a smaller print, but high quality.

   That's the largest size this photo can be printed at full quality. It was important to uncheck Resample (which means to add, remove, or recalculate pixels). We don't want to add/remove pixels. Instead, we're shrinking the pixels. At 300 ppi, pixels are too small to be seen. Refer to the sidebar at the end of the exercise for more info.

7. Click **OK**.

8. Go to **File > Save As**.

9. Use the following instructions to save this image as a **PSD** (**Photoshop Document**) or **TIFF**. What's the difference? PSD works great with other Adobe apps. TIFFs are more widely accepted in non-Adobe programs and often have slightly smaller file sizes if LZW compressed. Both maintain full image quality.

   Save As PSD

   1. Under **Format** (Mac) or **Save as type** (Windows), choose **Photoshop**.
   2. Name it **yourname-koala.psd** and click **Save**.
   3. If asked to maximize compatibility, leave it checked on and click **OK**.

   Save As TIFF

   1. Under **Format** (Mac) or **Save as type** (Windows), choose **TIFF**.
   2. Name it **yourname-koala.tif** and click **Save**.
   3. Set **Image Compression** to **LZW** then click **OK**. LZW is a lossless compression that shrinks file size while maintaining full image quality. It's widely accepted, but may not be compatible with all applications.

2G Photoshop: Preparing Digital Photos for Print

10. Close the file.

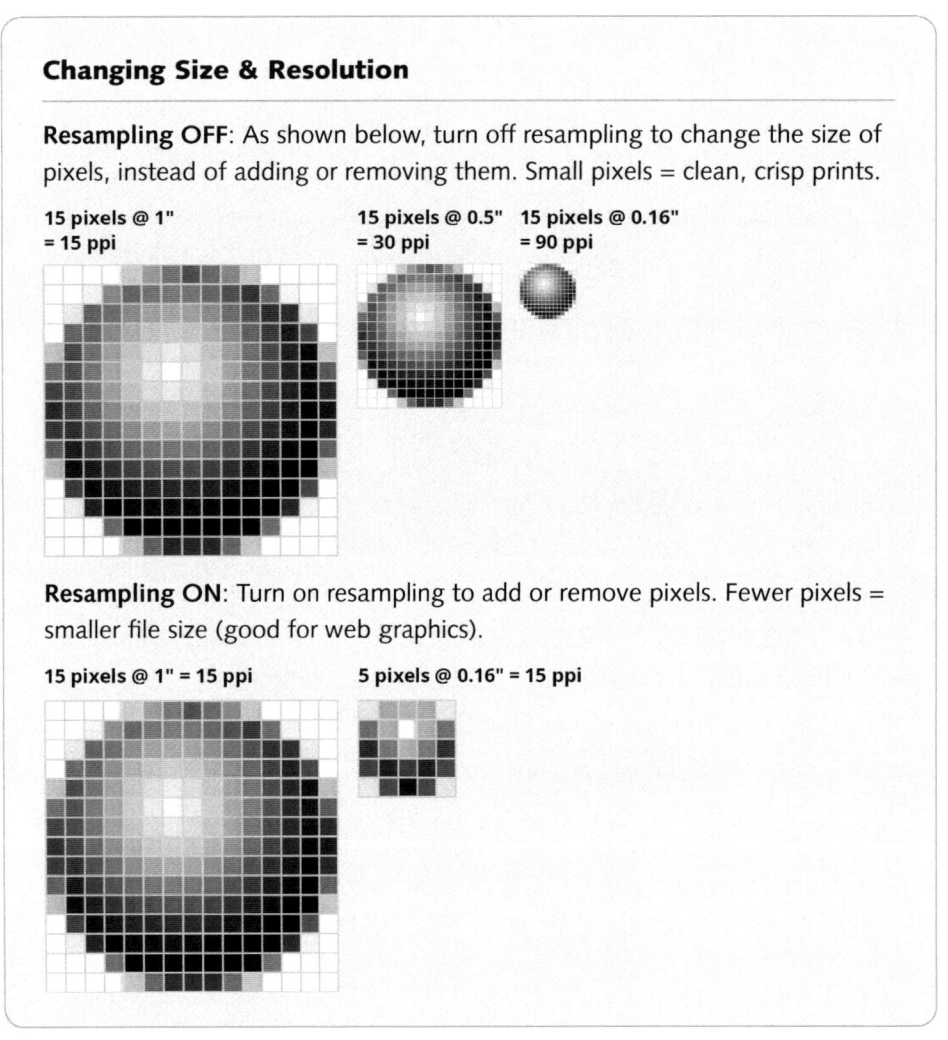

Photoshop: Saving Photos for the Web as JPEG

Exercise Preview

Exercise Overview

Many times, the same content will be used for both print and web and needs to be converted appropriately. Web images use RGB color and a resolution of 72 ppi, which corresponds to the number of pixels per inch that monitors display. Also, when you're saving images for the web, file size becomes an important issue. Larger files take longer to download!

Resizing an Image for the Web

1. From the **Photoshop Class** folder, open the file **opera house.tif**.

2. Before making this web-ready, it's a good practice to save a copy. Go to **File > Save As**.

3. Next to **Format** (Mac) or **Save as type** (Windows), choose **Photoshop**.

4. Name it **yourname-opera house-web.psd** and click **Save**. If changes are needed further on, you now have a clean original copy you can use to re-save for the web.

5. Go to **Image > Mode > RGB Color**.

6. Go to **Image > Image Size**.

7. Notice that the **Resolution** is 300. We need something less for the web.

2H Photoshop: Saving Photos for the Web as JPEG

8. At the bottom, check on **Resample**.

> **Resampling**
>
> **Resampling** means to **add**, **remove**, or **recalculate** pixels.
>
> When **Resample** is **checked**, the number of pixels actually changes. Either pixels are removed, creating an image with less pixel information, or pixels are added—these "made-up" pixels often result in a less detailed, more blurry image.
>
> When it is **unchecked**, resizing or changing the resolution of the image will not affect the number of pixels in the image—but you can convert a large printing, low-resolution image to a smaller printing, high-resolution version, or vice versa.

9. From the **Resample** menu, choose **Automatic**.

   Behind the scenes, Photoshop will automatically choose **Bicubic Sharper** because we'll be reducing the image's size. This helps maintain a bit more sharpness than **Bicubic**.

10. Next to Resolution, type **72**.

    Notice that the number of pixels have been reduced. We don't need all of them so resampling will throw out/recalculate the reduced number of pixels we need.

11. Make sure **Constrain Aspect Ratio** is depressed.

12. Set **Width** to **400** pixels, making sure to set **Pixels** as the units. The height will change automatically to maintain the proportions of the image.

13. Click **OK**.

Setting JPEG Quality in the Save for Web Dialog

1. Go to **File > Export > Save for Web (Legacy)**.

   NOTE: **Save for Web** is now marked as **Legacy** because Adobe won't be updating it to support new features such as artboards. In CC 2015 Adobe introduced brand new exporting methods such as **File > Export > Export As**. These new methods may be suitable in some cases, but they are currently not as developed and lack some options found in **Save for Web**. Adobe is keeping **Save for Web** until the new methods can fully replace it. For what we're doing in this book, we prefer **Save for Web** for its more complete feature set.

2. A new window appears, allowing you to adjust compression settings and preview the final image. Click the **4-Up** tab at the top.

Photoshop: Saving Photos for the Web as JPEG

2H

3. You're now looking at the original, uncompressed image in the upper left of the window, and three compressed versions, each using a different setting. Click on the **upper right** image.

4. In the settings on the right, from the menu **below Preset**, choose **JPEG**.

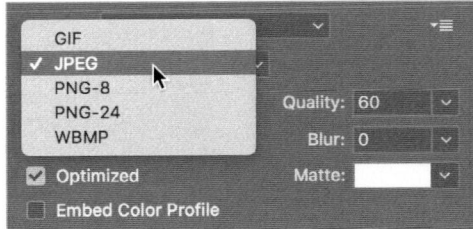

NOTE: The JPEG format is best for photos. It maintains good quality at a small file size. Be careful, though—the more you compress JPEGs, the more they will degrade and visual distortions will appear.

5. For the **Quality** setting on the right side of the window, type **100**.

    Note that the file size appears under each of the compressed preview images. While this doesn't cause much visual distortion, we can get a much smaller file if we try a lower quality.

6. Click on the **lower left** image. Choose **JPEG** and set the Quality to **0**.

    This is too distorted for most purposes, but the file size is small!

7. Click on the **lower right** image. Choose **JPEG** and set the Quality to **70**.

    This is getting closer. There's only minor distortion. The trade-off between quality and file size reaches a good balance here.

8. Notice that there's a thicker border around the **lower right** image preview area. That indicates it's the selected version. Click **Save** to save a copy of this one.

9. Make sure it's named **yourname-opera-house-web.jpg**.

    NOTE: When naming files for the web, DO NOT use spaces in the filename. Spaces will cause problems with web browsers. Use dashes or underscores instead. Photoshop will automatically replace any spaces with dashes.

10. Navigate to the **Photoshop Class** folder and click **Save** (Format: **Images Only**).

11. You should now be looking at the original Photoshop file. Go to **File > Save**. This will save the JPEG quality settings. So if changes need to be made later, it will remember the Save for Web settings we used for this specific file!

12. Close the file.

Photoshop: Saving Photos for the Web as GIF/PNG

Exercise Preview

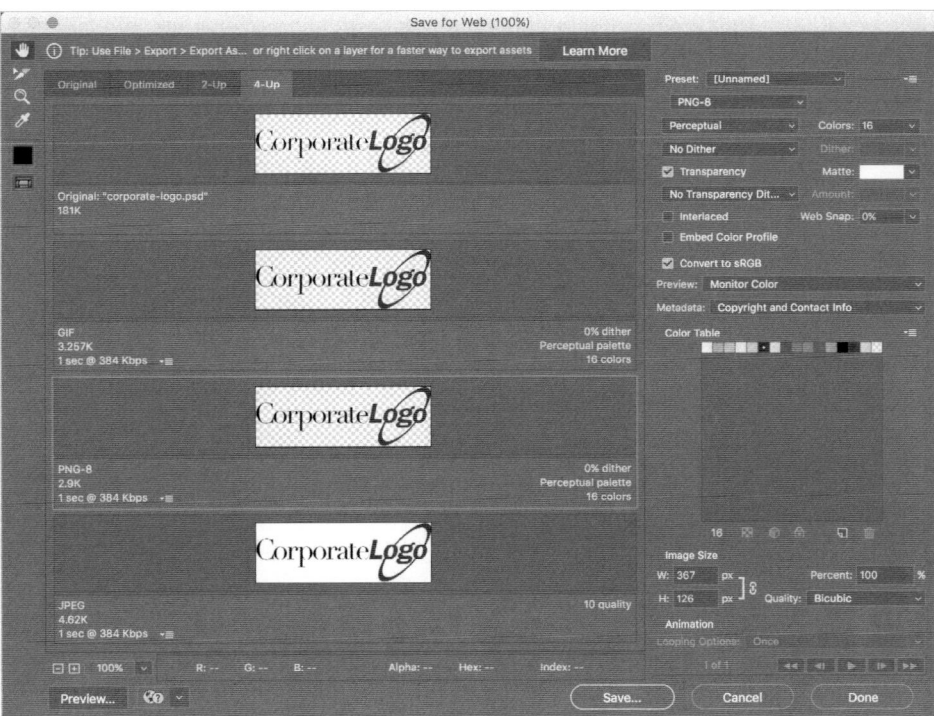

Exercise Overview

Photographs and images with many colors optimize better as JPEGs, but files with few colors (or areas of flat solid color) are ideal for GIF or PNG compression.

Saving as GIF

1. From the **Photoshop Class** folder, open the file **corporate-logo.psd**.

2. Although this image is already in **RGB** mode at **72 ppi**, we should crop out the empty pixels to make the file size smaller. We could use the **Crop** tool and trim it manually, but there's a better way. Go to **Image > Trim** and set the following:

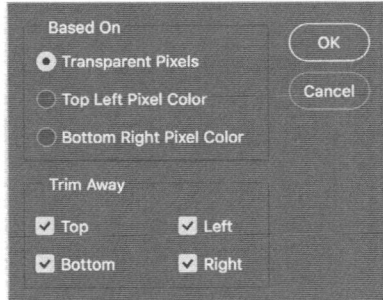

3. Click **OK**, and Photoshop quickly and precisely trims the image for you!

Photoshop: Saving Photos for the Web as GIF/PNG

4. Go to **File > Export > Save for Web (Legacy)**.

5. In the settings on the right, from the menu **below Preset**, choose **GIF**.

   The GIF format shrinks file size by reducing the total number of colors in an image. GIFs may have up to 256 colors, but generally you'll need far fewer than that.

6. From the **Colors** setting on the right, choose **16** Colors.

7. From the menu to the left of **Colors**, choose the **Perceptual** color palette.

   Adaptive, **Selective**, and **Perceptual** base their color choices on the actual image. The other options are preset color palettes and therefore are typically not desirable. We chose Perceptual in this case because it was the smallest file size, and visually there was almost no difference between the three options.

8. The **Dither** option uses scattered pixels to represent intermediate colors and often makes gradual blends look smoother. We don't need that in this image, so in the menu immediately below **Perceptual**, choose **No Dither**.

9. From the **Matte** menu, choose whatever color you'd want to use as the background of your imaginary website (in this case, white).

   GIF transparency does not allow for partial transparency. Therefore, any partially transparent pixels must become opaque. The Matte color is used as a background blend color for any pixels that are partially transparent in the original image. Choosing a color similar to your background allows the edges to better blend with the background of the webpage it will be used on.

10. Make sure that the **Transparency** checkbox is checked.

11. Choose the **Zoom** tool on the left side of the window.

12. Click on the image to zoom in. The formerly translucent pixels around the edge of the logo have been blended with the **Matte** color to form completely opaque pixels!

Comparing GIF to PNG-8

GIF and PNG-8 compressions work almost exactly the same, but PNG is newer. PNG files are often smaller than GIFs but not always. Since all the settings are the same, we can do a quick test right now to see which is better for this graphic.

1. Take note of the GIF's current file size.

2. In the settings on the right, from the menu **below** the **Preset**, change **GIF** to **PNG-8**.

3. Notice how the PNG is smaller? In our experience, a PNG with the same settings as a GIF is typically 5–25% smaller. For regular text, GIF is sometimes smaller, so you should typically do a test and go with whichever format yields a smaller file size.

Photoshop: Saving Photos for the Web as GIF/PNG

4. Click **Save** and save it as **yourname-logo.png** in the **Photoshop Class** folder.

Photoshop: Adjustment Layers & Masks   2J

Exercise Preview

BEFORE

AFTER

Exercise Overview

What a horribly washed-out image! We are going to make some color adjustments, but this time we'll use Adjustment Layers to gain more flexibility for future editing.

Adjusting Overall Colors & the Blue Channel

1. From the **Photoshop Class** folder, open the file **na pali coast.tif**.

2. Go to **View > Fit on Screen** (**Cmd–0** (Mac) or **Ctrl–0** (Windows)).

3. At the bottom of the **Layers** panel, click on **Create new fill or adjustment layer**, and from the menu, choose **Curves**.

4. You will see the curves open in the **Properties** panel, as shown below. You may need to resize the window to see all these options.

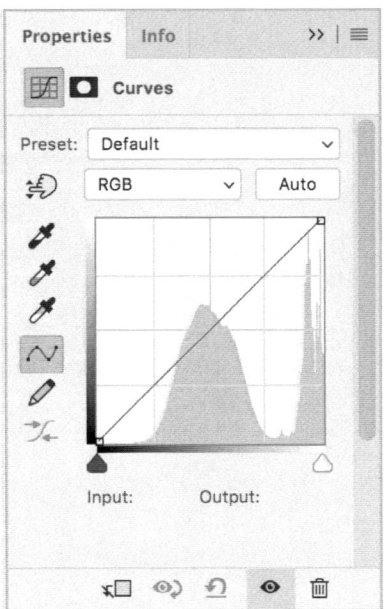

ADOBE CREATIVE CLOUD 2018 • COPYRIGHT NOBLE DESKTOP

2J Photoshop: Adjustment Layers & Masks

5. Most of the screenshots in this exercise show Photoshop's lightest interface instead of the default medium dark interface. Throughout the book, we may use the light interface when it improves the print quality. (Interface brightness can be changed by going into the **Photoshop CC** menu (Mac) or **Edit** menu (Windows), choosing **Preferences > Interface**, and clicking on the desired **Color Theme**.)

6. Now we are ready to do some color correction. Let's start by properly setting our white and black points, then adjusting the contrast. Look at the histogram and notice in the bottom-left corner that it has no peaks. This means there are no pixels that are black or very dark gray.

7. As shown below, to fix this, hold **Option** (Mac) or **Alt** (Windows) while you drag the **Black** point slider 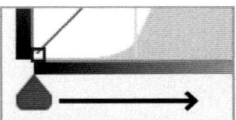 to the right.

   The image will turn white, but as you get close to the beginning of the histogram's "hill," some small pixels will start to appear in various colors. When you see a few of the colored pixels appear, stop dragging. Those pixels have now been set to black.

8. The photo looks a little cool and bluish. At the top of the **Properties** panel, where it now says **RGB**, choose **Blue** as shown below.

9. Click in the center of the curve and **drag down** a bit to take out some of the blue.

   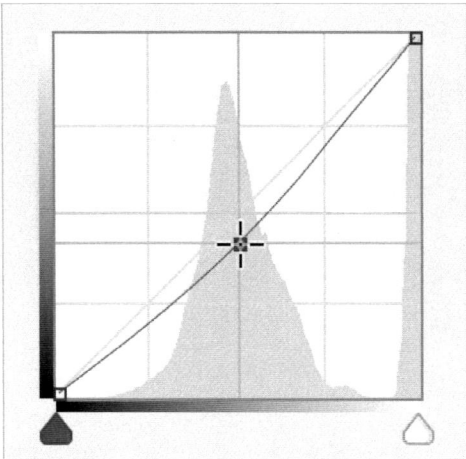

Photoshop: Adjustment Layers & Masks

10. In the **Layers** panel, double–click on **Curves 1** and rename it **contrast & color**.

11. The sky is still too bright, but the rest looks good. At the bottom of the **Layers** panel, click on **Create new fill or adjustment layer** and choose **Curves**.

12. Looking at just the sky for reference, make the following adjustment:

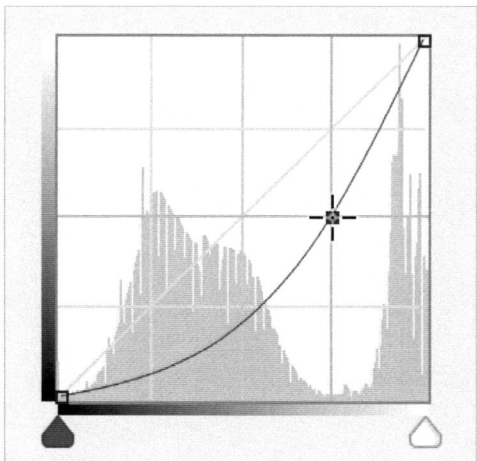

Make sure that the sky looks good, and don't worry about the land. We'll be hiding (masking out) any unwanted areas in a moment.

13. In the **Layers** panel, double–click **Curves 1** and rename it **sky**.

Masking Out Unwanted Adjustments

1. In the **sky** layer, click the **layer mask thumbnail** so it is highlighted, as shown below. You will see that it is highlighted when brackets appear around the empty white box. We are going to edit this layer mask.

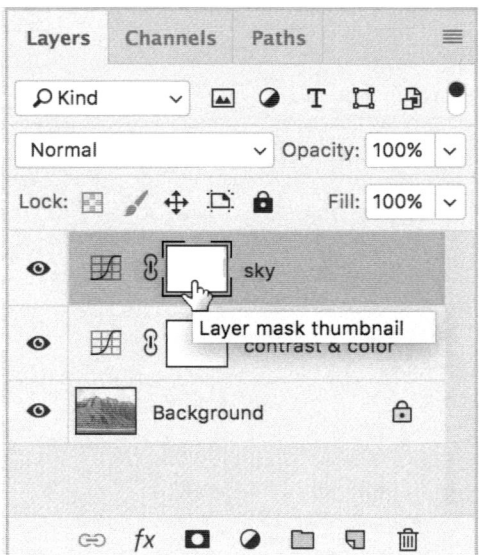

Photoshop: Adjustment Layers & Masks

2. Choose the **Gradient** tool.

3. At the left of the **Options** bar, click the arrow next to the gradient preview to open the gradient panel, and double–click the **third** thumbnail on the left in the top row, which is the **Black, White** gradient.

4. Also in the **Options** bar, choose:

   - **Linear Gradient**
   - Mode: **Normal**
   - Opacity: **100%**
   - **Dither** and **Transparency** should be checked.

5. Starting one third of the way up from the bottom (around the brown dirt), drag **up** to the top of the mountain range.

6. The black on the mask has hidden the darkening effect of this adjustment layer at the bottom, and the mask's white has made it visible at the top. There may be parts we want to darken or lighten. Choose the **Brush** tool.

7. In the **Tools** panel, click the **Default Colors** icon.

8. In the **Options** bar, choose a huge brush (at least **250 px**) with **0% hardness**.

9. Also in the **Options** bar, lower the **Opacity** to **20%**.

10. Painting white with a 20% Opacity on the mask will slowly reveal the darker **sky** curves adjustment. Paint anywhere that looks a little bright to darken it a bit.

11. Likewise, press **X** to swap the Foreground and Background colors so you have **black**. Now paint anywhere that looks too dark to mask that layer and brighten it up.

Organizing Layers into Groups

We want to see what the image looks like without our adjustments to get a sense of what we've done, but before doing that, let's do one more thing to jazz up this photo. We want that Hawaiian foliage to really pop out!

1. At the bottom of the **Layers** panel, click on **Create new fill or adjustment layer**, and from the menu, choose **Hue/Saturation**.

2. In the **Properties** panel, move the **Saturation** slider to the right to somewhere between **10–20**. Experiment with what you think looks best. We want to add color but not make it look fake.

3. We'd like to compare the final image to the original. A nice way to do this (and keep the file organized) is to put the layers into a Layer Group. In the **Layers** panel, make sure the top layer is still selected.

Photoshop: Adjustment Layers & Masks

4. Hold **Shift** and click on the **contrast & color** layer. All three adjustment layers should now be selected.

5. Go into **Layer > Group Layers** (**Cmd–G** (Mac) or **Ctrl–G** (Windows)).

6. In the **Layers** panel, you should now see a folder. Double–click the folder's name and change it to **my adjustments**.

7. Click the **arrow** to the left of the **my adjustments** layer group to expand it and see that your layers are inside.

8. Click the **eye** beside the **my adjustments** layer group a few times to hide and show all the layers it contains. This lets you see a before and after. Pow!

    When you see the background layer without the effect of the adjustment layers, it's clear that the original layer is unchanged. Adjustment layers allow flexibility of editing, and they preserve the original image!

9. **File > Save As** as **yourname-na pali coast.psd**, setting **Format** (Mac) or **Save as type** (Windows) to **Photoshop** to maintain layer editability.

Photoshop: Using Layer Masks for Silhouettes

2K

Exercise Preview

Exercise Overview

We will use a Layer Mask to remove the background from around a picture of a hat. Layer Masks offer the most editing flexibility and they are non-destructive. This exercise also involves importing into InDesign. You can do most of the steps if you don't have InDesign, but you will not be able to finish the exercise.

Selecting the Hat

1. From the **Photoshop Class** folder, open the image **hat.tif**.

    Notice how part of the hat's brim is not in focus, and some areas of the background are a similar color to the hat. With a combination of selection tools and layer masks, even a challenging silhouetting task like this is a piece of cake!

2. Choose the **Magnetic Lasso** tool.

3. In the **Options** bar, make sure it has the following settings:

    Feather: **0 px**
    Width: **10 px**
    Contrast: **10%**
    Frequency: **57**

4. Click **once** along the brim to start the lasso selection. (Do not click and hold.)

Photoshop: Using Layer Masks for Silhouettes

5. Move the cursor along the edges of the hat, and the lasso will lay down points along the path as the cursor moves. Keep in mind the following tips:

    - When you reach a corner or tricky place, click to manually place a point.
    - Press **Delete** (Mac) or **Backspace** (Windows) to back up and delete points that have been placed incorrectly.

6. When you reach the end, place the cursor over the first point, so it changes to a ⊘ and click to finish the selection.

7. In the **Options** bar, click the **Select and Mask** button.

8. In the **Properties** panel on the right, click on the thumbnail next to **View** and double–click **On Black**.

9. Set **Opacity** to **100%**.

10. In the **Edge Detection** section, make sure **Radius** is set to **0 px**.

11. In the **Global Refinements** section, set the following:

    Smooth: **10**
    Feather: **0.5 px**
    Contrast: **0%**
    Shift Edge: Around **–40%**, but experiment with what looks best for you.

12. In the **Output Settings** section, make sure **Output To** is set to **Layer Mask**.

13. Click **OK**.

14. In the **Layers** panel, notice the Background layer has been changed into a regular layer with a new name (**Layer 0**) and a layer mask has been added.

    NOTE: Background layers cannot be transparent or have layer masks, so the **Select and Mask** feature converted it into a normal layer for us!

15. In the **Layers** panel, double–click the **Layer 0** layer and name it **hat**.

16. At the bottom of the **Layers** panel, click the **Create new fill or adjustment layer** button, and from the menu, choose **Solid Color**.

17. Choose **black** and click **OK**.

18. In the **Layers** panel, click and drag the **Color Fill 1** layer below the **hat** layer.

Cleaning Up the Edges

There may be spots showing through from the old background, and the brim edge should be softer. Let's start by fixing the top part of the hat. Later we'll fix the brim.

1. In the **Layers** panel, double–click the **Color Fill 1** layer's thumbnail.

Photoshop: Using Layer Masks for Silhouettes

2. Set the following RGB values:

   R: **0**
   G: **70**
   B: **100**

3. Click **OK**.

4. In the **Layers** panel, click the hat layer mask.

5. Select the **Brush** tool.

6. In the **Options** bar, choose a **small-sized**, **fairly hard** brush. We recommend about **8 px diameter** and **90% hardness**. This size will let you get into the corners nicely.

   Make sure **Opacity** and **Flow** are set to **100%**.

7. Press **D** to set the default white and black foreground and background colors.

8. Press the **X** key to switch the foreground/background colors so the foreground color is **black**.

9. Paint over areas where you see the original light background color around the hat (zoom in as needed). This will remove it, kind of like you are erasing it.

10. As needed, reduce the brush size to get into corners, etc.

11. If you removed any parts of the hat and want to reveal them, remember:

    - Paint **white** over any parts you want to reveal (like the hat).
    - Paint **black** over any parts you want to hide (like the background).
    - Press the **X** key to switch the foreground and background colors.

Finishing Up

The front and back of the brim are blurry in the photo, but the edge of our mask makes them look crisp.

1. Select the **Blur** tool.

2. In the **Options** bar, choose a **medium-sized soft brush** (about **40 px, 0% hardness**).

3. Click and drag to blur the edges of the brim in the front and back.

4. In the **Layers** panel, select the **Color Fill 1** layer.

5. Drag it to the **Trash** button to delete it. Now you should be left with a transparent checkerboard background.

2K Photoshop: Using Layer Masks for Silhouettes

Importing the Image into InDesign

To save this file, we need to choose a file format appropriate for InDesign.

1. Go to **File > Save As**.

2. Navigate into the **Kissimmee Brochure** folder (inside the **Photoshop Class** folder).

3. Set **Format** (Mac) or **Save as type** (Windows) to **Photoshop** and name the image **yourname-hat.psd**. Click **Save**.

   NOTE: TIFF can also work, but you must check on **Save Transparency**.

4. Launch **InDesign** (if you have more than one version, launch **CC 2018**).

5. From the **Kissimmee Brochure** folder, open the InDesign file **Brochure-add hat.indd**.

6. Choose the **Selection tool**.

7. On the bottom left, click on the empty rectangular picture box.

8. Go to **File > Place**.

9. Choose **yourname-hat.psd** and click **Open**.

10. Go to **View > Display Performance > High Quality Display**.

11. Zoom in and examine the blurry, semi-transparent parts. Very nice.

    Enjoy your work—you're done! Because we no longer need this file, close the InDesign file and do NOT save changes.

Illustrator Preferences: Do Before Remaining Exercises! 3A

Exercise Overview

To get started with Adobe Illustrator, you'll need to do some setup first. It's important to do this exercise, or the Illustrator exercises in this book will not work correctly!

Setting Preferences

1. Launch **Adobe Illustrator**.

    NOTE: The Illustrator exercises in this book have been tested with **Illustrator CC 2018**.

2. Go into the **Illustrator CC** menu (Mac) or the **Edit** menu (Windows) and choose **Preferences > Selection & Anchor Display**.

3. Make the changes to match the settings below:

    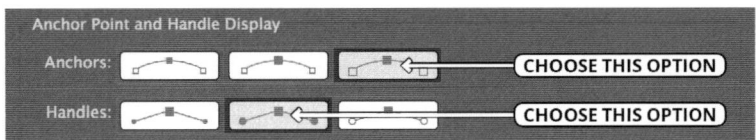

4. Click **OK**. This changes the size of anchor points and handles. Enlarging them makes finding and selecting them easier. This preference will remain for future files.

5. Go to the **View** menu. If **Smart Guides** is checked, choose it to **uncheck** it.

Cleaning Up the Interface

1. Let's make sure your interface is set up the same way as this book assumes. Go to **Window > Workspace > Essentials**.

2. Go to **Window > Workspace > Reset Essentials** to reset the panels to their default locations.

3. The **Control** panel shows useful settings and makes Illustrator more like Photoshop and InDesign. Go into **Window > Control**, and the panel will open at the top of the interface.

4. If there is a large **Libraries** panel on the right side of the screen, close it by choosing **Window > Libraries**.

Illustrator: Straight Lines

Exercise Preview

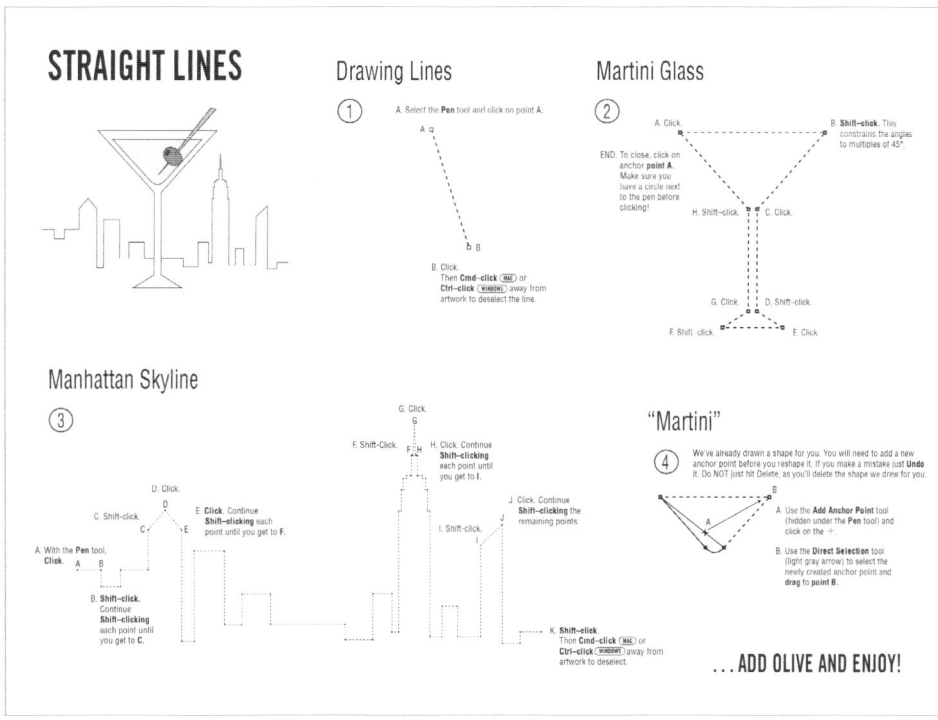

Exercise Overview

The **Pen** tool is the heart of Illustrator. This exercise gets you started drawing simple lines and shapes.

Getting Started

1. Go to **File > Open**.

2. Navigate to the **Desktop**, then into the **Class Files** folder, then into the **Illustrator Class** folder. Open the **Straight Lines Template.ai** file.

3. Select **File > Save As**.

4. At the bottom, make sure **Format** (Mac) or **Save as type** (Windows) is set to **Adobe Illustrator** (**ai**).

5. Navigate into the same **Illustrator Class** folder you opened it from.

6. Name the file **yourname-Straight Lines.ai**.

7. Click **Save**.

8. In the dialog that appears, leave the default options checked and click **OK**.

3B Illustrator: Straight Lines

Selecting Colors & Using the Template

1. As shown below, toward the bottom of the **Tools** panel, click the **Default Fill and Stroke** button . This makes your fill white and the stroke black.

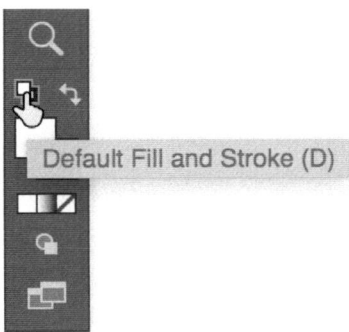

2. As shown below, click the **Fill** icon to make it active.

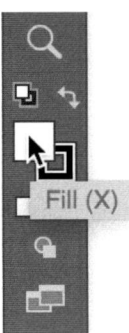

3. Click the **None** button just below that.

4. Follow the on-screen directions in the file. When you have completed the directions, save your changes and move on to the next steps below.

Finishing Up Once You're Done with the Template

You've drawn all the shapes for the Manhattan Martini image, so let's arrange them.

1. Using the **Selection** tool , click on the **Glass** you drew.

2. **Shift–click** the **Martini** and the **Manhattan Skyline** shape.

3. Now that all three shapes are selected, copy them (**Edit > Copy**).

4. Go to **File > Open** and from the **Illustrator Class** folder, choose **Manhattan Martini.ai**.

5. Paste the objects (**Edit > Paste**).

6. We've included the **Olive** and **Toothpick** for you. You will learn how to draw curved lines in an upcoming exercise, but we've provided these shapes for now.

Illustrator: Straight Lines

7. Click away from the artwork to deselect it.

8. Let's arrange things starting with the **Glass**. With the **Selection** tool, click and hold **directly** on **one of its lines** and drag it to the **center** of the page.

Coloring the Martini Glass

1. In the docked panels at the right of the screen, make sure you are in the **Properties** panel. If you aren't, click on the tab name or go to **Window > Properties**.

2. This shape needs a **white** fill. With the **Glass** still selected, go to the **Properties** panel and under **Appearance**, click on the swatch next to **Fill**. (It should look like .)

   NOTE: Prior to CC 2018, there was no Properties panel. Activate the Fill in the **Tools** panel and use the **Color** panel (**Window > Color**) instead.

3. At the top middle of the panel that appears, click the **Color Mixer** button if it isn't already selected.

4. Choose **white** by clicking on the white swatch towards the bottom left of the Color Mixer panel above the color bar.

5. To close the Color Mixer panel, press **Return** (Mac) or **Enter** (Windows).

6. Click on the **Martini** shape and place it inside the glass… and while it's still selected, choose **Object > Arrange > Bring to Front**.

   A light blue color would make a refreshing-looking "Martini." Let's fill it with color.

7. In the **Properties** panel next to **Appearance**, click on the **Fill** icon.

8. We want to have maximum precision when choosing colors, so we will use the **CMYK** color sliders. If the **Color Mixer** panel isn't showing **CMYK** color sliders, go into the **panel menu** at the top right of the panel and choose **CMYK**.

9. The first line is **C** (**C** stands for **C**yan). Type **7** in the box at the end of this line and press **Tab**.

10. If the other 3 colors (**MYK**) don't all become **0**, then make them **0**.

11. To close the Color Mixer panel, press **Return** (Mac) or **Enter** (Windows).

Arranging the Other Elements

1. Click on the **Manhattan Skyline** and place it behind the glass.

2. Notice that the line of the Skyline is on top of the glass. With the Skyline still selected, choose **Object > Arrange > Send to Back**.

3B Illustrator: Straight Lines

3. The Skyline is too big compared to the glass. With the shape still selected, go to the **Tools** panel and double–click the **Scale** tool.

4. In the dialog box that appears, for **Uniform** Scale, enter **75%** and click **OK**.

5. Reposition the Skyline if needed. Make sure to choose the **Selection** tool.

6. On the **top-right** corner of the page, find the three shapes that make up the **Olive and Toothpick**.

7. Stay in that corner and use the **Selection** tool to assemble the shapes so the toothpick is touching/poking through the olive.

8. **Shift–click** all three shapes and go to **Object > Group**.

9. With the olive and pick still selected, choose **Object > Arrange > Bring to Front**.

10. Move the olive and pick onto the Martini Glass.

11. Select **File > Save As** and name it **yourname-Manhattan Martini.ai**.

12. Hit **Save**. In the dialog that appears, leave the default options checked and click **OK**.

Saving Illustrator Files

Once you click the **Save** button, an Options dialog will appear. You should keep the **Version** set to the version of Illustrator you are currently using (in our case, that's **Illustrator CC**).

If you will need to edit the file with an older version of Illustrator, you can save back to an older version, but be careful. Newer features may not translate properly to older versions.

Create PDF Compatible File should be checked on (as it is by default) to ensure the best compatibility with other Creative Cloud applications such as InDesign and Photoshop.

Embed ICC Profiles is an advanced topic since it relates to a color managed workflow. For now, don't worry about it and just stick with whatever your default is (on or off).

Use Compression should be checked on to reduce file size (without loss of quality).

Illustrator: Curves

Exercise Preview

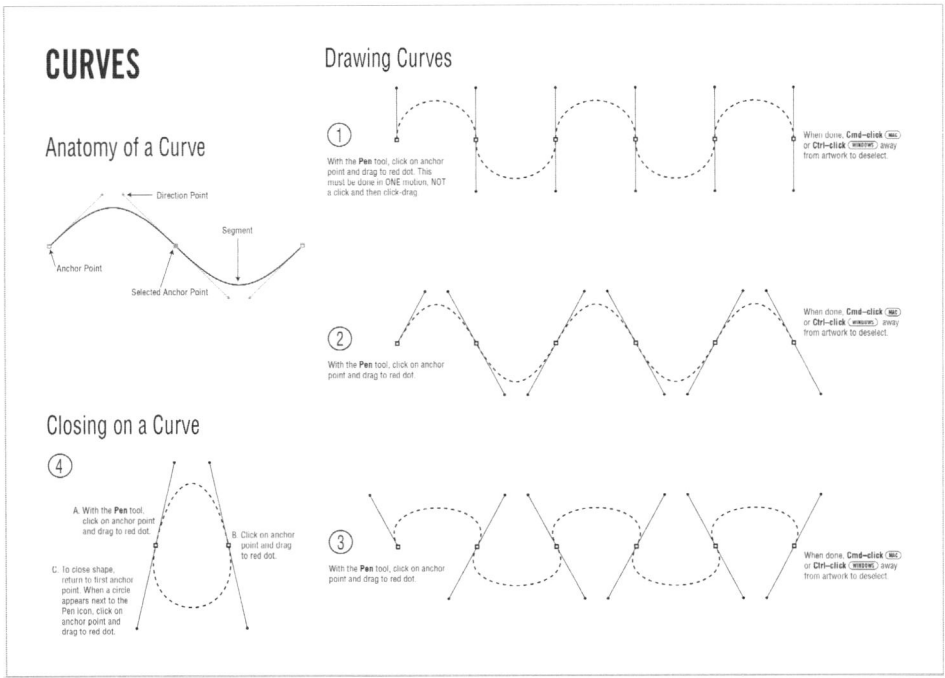

Exercise Overview

Continuing in our quest for mastery of the **Pen** tool , this exercise walks you through creating curved lines and shapes.

1. From the **Illustrator Class** folder, open the file **Curves Template.ai**.

2. Select **File > Save As**, naming the file **yourname-Curves.ai**.

3. Click **Save**. In the dialog that appears, leave the default options checked and click **OK**.

4. In the **Tools** panel, click the **Default Fill and Stroke** button .

5. In the **Tools** panel, click the **Fill** icon and then click the **None** button .

6. Follow the on-screen directions in the file. When you have completed the directions, **File > Save** your changes.

Illustrator: Corners & Curves

Exercise Preview

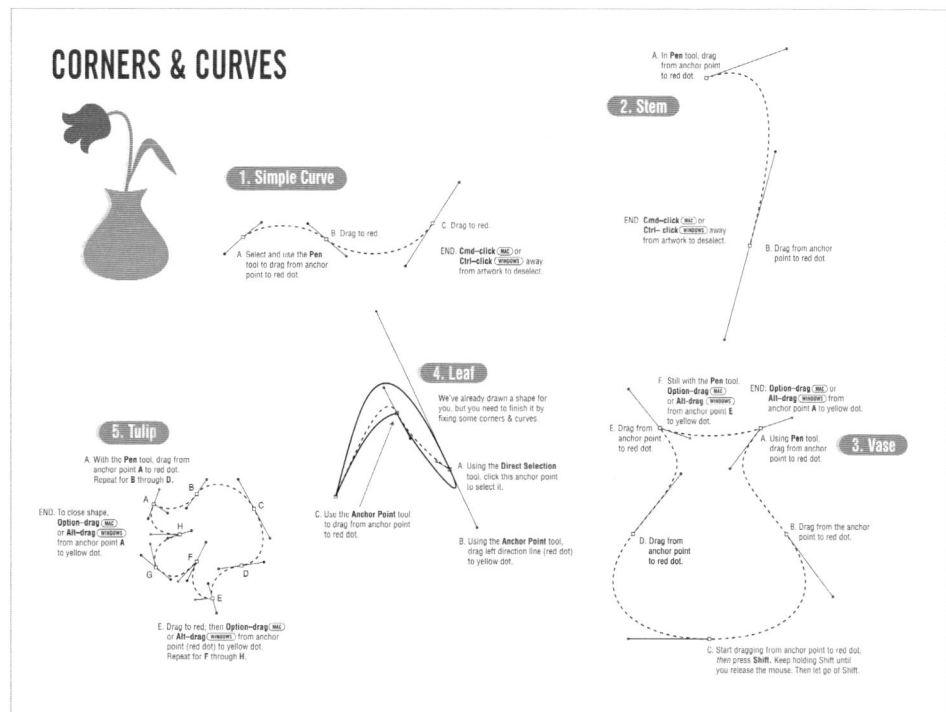

Exercise Overview

Corners can be tricky to draw, but this template walks you through drawing them and makes it quite easy.

1. From the **Illustrator Class** folder, open the file **Corners & Curves Template.ai**.
2. Select **File > Save As**, naming the file **yourname-Corners & Curves.ai**.
3. Click **Save**.
4. In the dialog that appears, leave the default options checked and click **OK**.

Selecting Colors & Using the Template

1. In the **Tools** panel, click the **Default Fill and Stroke** button.
2. In the **Tools** panel, click the **Fill** icon and then click the **None** button.
3. Follow the on-screen directions in the file. When you have completed the directions, save your changes and move on to the next section in this exercise.

3D Illustrator: Corners & Curves

Finishing Up Once You're Done with the Template

You've drawn the shapes that make up the complete image of the vase and flower, so let's put them all together.

1. If you closed the **yourname-Corners & Curves.ai** file, please open it again.
2. Using the **Selection** tool , click on the **Stem** you drew.
3. **Shift–click** the **Vase**, **Leaf**, and **Tulip** so they are also selected.
4. Now that all four shapes are selected, copy them (**Edit > Copy**).
5. Go to **File > New** to create a new document.
6. At the top of the dialog that opens, click on the **Print** tab.
7. Double–click the **Letter** preset to open the new file.
8. Select **File > Save**, naming the file **yourname-flowers.ai**.
9. Click **Save**, and in the dialog that appears, click **OK**.
10. Now paste your objects (**Edit > Paste**).
11. Click away from the artwork to deselect the shapes.
12. The shapes need to be arranged. Let's start with the **Vase**. Using the **Selection** tool , drag it by one of its lines to the center of the page.
13. Drag the **Stem** into place above the Vase.
14. Drag the **Tulip** to the end of the Stem.
15. Drag the **Leaf** into place above the Vase and to the right of the Stem.
16. Click away from the artwork to deselect the shapes. The composition is now complete, but some color would really enhance this.
17. Click on the **Vase** to select it.
18. Click on the **Fill** icon (in the **Tools** panel).
19. In the **Properties** panel under **Appearance**, click on the swatch next to **Fill**.
20. In the **Color Mixer** panel, enter **60** next to **M** (**M**agenta) and **90** next to **Y** (**Y**ellow). **C**yan and blac**K** should remain at **0**.

    For the rest of this workbook, when we ask you to enter **CMYK** values, we will use a shorthand direction. The above values would be written **60m** and **90y**.

21. To close the Color Mixer panel, press **Return** (Mac) or **Enter** (Windows).
22. Click on the **Tulip** to select it.

Illustrator: Corners & Curves

23. In the **Properties** panel, click on the **Fill** icon. Then in the **Color Mixer** panel, enter **7c** and **94m**.

    NOTE: When you type in color values, Illustrator will sometimes reinsert the values from the last color you specified into the remaining fields. So for any color values you are not specifying, be sure to make them **0** if Illustrator didn't.

24. To close the Color Mixer panel, press **Return** (Mac) or **Enter** (Windows).

25. Click on the **Leaf** to select it.

26. In the **Properties** panel, click on the **Fill** icon. Then in the **Color Mixer** panel, enter **66c** and **100y**.

    NOTE: Once you click in a number field in the **Color Mixer** panel, just hit **Tab** to jump to the field below. This makes entering numbers for colors faster!

27. To close the Color Mixer panel, press **Return** (Mac) or **Enter** (Windows).

28. Click on the **Stem** to select it.

    The Stem and Leaf should both be the same green. The Stem is just a line, so it needs a stroke color, not a fill color.

29. In the **Properties** panel under **Appearance**, click on the swatch next to **Stroke**. (It should be a black outline.)

30. At the top middle of the panel that appears, click the **Color Mixer** button if it isn't already selected.

31. In the **Color Mixer** panel, enter **66c** and **100y**.

32. To close the Color Mixer panel, press **Return** (Mac) or **Enter** (Windows).

33. With the Stem still selected, go back to the **Properties** panel and in the menu to the right of the **Stroke** swatch, change the weight from 1 pt to **5 pt**.

    TIP: You can also do this in the **Control** panel at the top of the screen.

34. Let's get rid of those black strokes on everything else.

    With the **Selection** tool, starting outside the shapes, click and drag a selection marquee over everything. When you let go, they will be selected.

35. **Shift–click** the **Stem** to deselect it. (Because the stem only consists of a line, it would disappear if we removed its stroke!)

3D Illustrator: Corners & Curves

36. In the **Tools** panel, make sure that the **Stroke** icon is active and is black. If it is showing question marks, the stem is probably still selected.

   > **Question Marks?**
   >
   > When multiple objects are selected, sometimes the Stroke and Fill icons show question marks.
   >
   >
   >
   > This means that there are multiple Fill or Stroke colors for those objects. Illustrator doesn't know which color to show. If they are all the same color, Illustrator will show that color.

37. Click the **None** button.

38. Click off the artwork to deselect it.

39. Select **File > Save** and close the file.

   Spring has sprung!

Illustrator: No Smoking Sign

3E

Exercise Preview

Exercise Overview

Here you'll get more practice drawing and creating strokes and fills. You will also learn about the incredibly important and useful Layers panel.

Getting Started

1. Go to **File > New** to create a new document.

2. At the top of the dialog that opens, click on the **Print** tab.

3. Double–click the **Letter** preset.

4. Select **File > Save As**, naming the document **yourname-No Smoking.ai**.

5. Click **Save**. In the dialog that appears, leave the default options checked and click **OK**.

6. Go to **View > Fit Artboard in Window**.

7. Go to **File > Place**.

8. In the **Illustrator Class** folder, click on **NoSmoking.tif** to select it, and then at the bottom of the window, check **Template** (Mac users may need to click the **Options** button).

9. Click **Place**.

10. In the tabs at the top right, to the right of the **Properties** panel name, click on the word **Layers** to switch to that panel. (If you can't find it, go to **Window > Layers**.)

3E Illustrator: No Smoking Sign

11. In the **Layers** panel, there are now two layers. The **Template NoSmoking.tif** layer holds the file you placed and it is automatically locked so you don't edit it accidentally. You will do the tracing on **Layer 1**, which is already selected as the active layer.

12. Go to **View > Rulers > Show Rulers**.

13. From the top ruler, click and drag down a guide into the center of the circle.

14. From the left ruler, click and drag out another guide into the center of the circle.

15. To make sure the guides are locked, go to **View > Guides**. If you see **Unlock Guides**, you're good to go! If you instead see **Lock Guides**, click that option now.

Drawing the Circle & Slash Line

1. Select the **Ellipse** tool. If you don't see it, click and hold on the **Rectangle** tool to get it.

2. Hold down **Option–Shift** (Mac) or **Alt–Shift** (Windows), and **click and drag** from the **center point** where the guides meet to the **edges of the circle**.

   NOTE: Holding **Option** (Mac) or **Alt** (Windows) makes any shape (including this ellipse) draw out from the center point. Holding **Shift** constrains the oval's proportions to make it a perfect circle.

3. We want to change the stroke to red, so go to the top right and click on the **Properties** panel name to switch to it.

4. In the **Properties** panel under **Appearance**, click on the swatch next to **Stroke**.

5. Make the color **100m**, **100y**. (If the Color Mixer panel is not displaying CMYK, go into the **panel menu** at the upper right of the panel and choose **CMYK**.) Make sure **C** and **K** are set to **0**.

6. To close the Color Mixer panel, press **Return** (Mac) or **Enter** (Windows).

7. With the circle still selected, go back to the **Properties** panel and in the menu to the right of the **Stroke** swatch, change the weight from 1 pt to **19 pt**.

   NOTE: You can also enter Stroke weight in the **Control** panel at the top of the screen or the **Stroke** panel (**Window > Stroke**).

8. Right now you are working in **Preview** mode, and you have covered the template by filling the circle. To see the template, go to **View > Outline**.

9. Go to **Select > Deselect**.

10. Select the **Line Segment** tool.

Illustrator: No Smoking Sign

11. Hold down **Option–Shift** (Mac) or **Alt–Shift** (Windows) and **click and drag** from the **center point** to the **edge of the circle**, following the template.

    NOTE: Holding **Shift** constrains the line to a 90° or 45° angle.

12. Keep the line selected and switch to **Preview** mode by choosing either **View > GPU Preview** or **View > Preview**.

    The line should already be the proper red color and thickness because it kept the settings you just used.

    NOTE: Preview on GPU will only be available if you have a supported graphics card.

13. If you have the GPU Preview option, there are two ways to preview (GPU and CPU). The GPU Preview should be faster than the CPU Preview, but it might not look as good. To switch back and forth between the GPU and CPU previews, press **Cmd–E** (Mac) or **Ctrl–E** (Windows) a few times. As you switch, look at the smoothness of edges. You can tell which type of preview you're using by looking in the tab at the top of the window that contains the filename. Use whichever looks better.

14. Go to **Select > Deselect**.

Drawing the Cigarette

1. Before we start to draw the cigarette, we don't want to use the big red stroke we currently have. In the **Tools** panel, click **Default Fill and Stroke**.

2. Trace over the cigarette using the **Rectangle** tool for both parts. If you don't see it, click and hold on the **Ellipse** tool to get it.

    NOTE: If the Transform panel opens up when you draw a rectangle, click on the **Transform panel menu** and uncheck **Show on Shape Creation** to turn this off.

3. With the **Selection** tool, select the rectangle that forms the tip of the cigarette.

4. In the **Properties** panel under **Appearance**, click on the swatch next to **Fill**.

5. You are going to color the cigarette using color swatches. At the top middle of the Color Mixer panel, click the **Swatches** button to switch to the Swatches panel.

    NOTE: In Illustrator CC 2017 and older, we used the standalone Swatches panel found in **Window > Swatches**.

6. Give it a black fill by clicking on the **black** swatch in the **Swatches** panel.

7. To close the Swatches panel, press **Return** (Mac) or **Enter** (Windows).

8. Let's change the stroke width. Go back to the **Properties** panel and in the menu to the right of the **Stroke** swatch, set the weight to **3 pt**.

9. Select the left part of the cigarette and give it a **3 pt black** stroke.

3E Illustrator: No Smoking Sign

10. The next thing we need to do is trace the smoke. However, any lines we draw right now would have a black fill. Deselect all, click on the **Fill** icon, and choose **None**.

11. Switch into **Outline** mode to draw the smoke. The fastest way to do this is to hit **Cmd–Y** (Mac) or **Ctrl–Y** (Windows).

12. Zoom in (using the **Zoom** tool or **View > Zoom In**) so the smoke fills more of the screen. Just make sure you can still see all of it.

13. Trace the smoke using the **Pen** tool.

14. Let's see how things are looking. Hit **Cmd–Y** (Mac) or **Ctrl–Y** (Windows) to switch back to **Preview** mode.

    NOTE: This keystroke will default to the preview type (GPU or CPU) that you last used, although it's not remembered across files.

15. Make sure both smoke paths have a **3 pt black Stroke** and **Fill** set to **None**.

Putting It All Together

1. Use the **Selection** tool to select all parts of the **cigarette**, including the smoke, by **Shift–clicking** or by clicking and dragging a marquee around them.

2. Group the cigarette parts using **Object > Group**.

3. Move the cigarette group into the center of the circle.

   Wait! Alas, the cigarette is in front of the sign! To fix this, you are now going to paste the cigarette in back of the slash.

4. Cut the cigarette group (**Edit > Cut**).

5. Select the rotated line, or slash. (You have to click on the actual path in the middle of the big stroke to select it. It may be easier to select it in **Outline** mode.)

6. Choose **Edit > Paste in Back**.

Adding a Frame

1. To switch back to **Outline** mode so you can see the template, hit **Cmd–Y** (Mac) or **Ctrl–Y** (Windows).

2. Select the **Rounded Rectangle** tool (if you don't see it, click and hold on the **Rectangle** tool to get to it).

3. Hold down **Option** (Mac) or **Alt** (Windows) and click once in the **center** of the circle. It's important just to click (do NOT hold down or drag the mouse) to bring up the dialog box for precise drawing.

Illustrator: No Smoking Sign

4. In the dialog that appears, enter the following measurements:

   Width: **194 pt**
   Height: **194 pt**
   Corner Radius: **15 pt**

5. Click **OK**.

6. Switch back to **Preview** mode (**Cmd–Y** (Mac) or **Ctrl–Y** (Windows)) and give the rounded square a **white** fill and **3 pt black** stroke.

7. Since the fill obscures the other objects, with the rounded square selected, choose **Object > Arrange > Send to Back**.

8. It looks pretty good, but the template is still showing. To hide it, look at the **Layers** panel. Notice the **Template NoSmoking.tif** layer. As shown below, click on the visibility icon to its left to hide it.

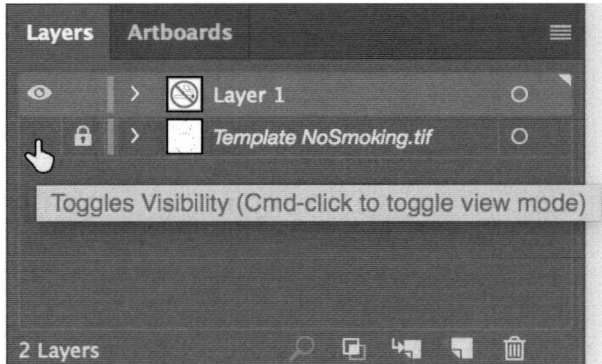

9. Go to **View > Guides > Hide Guides**.

10. Congratulations! You're done. **Save** your changes and print it if you wish.

Illustrator: Super Hero

Exercise Preview

Exercise Overview

Often you'll want to take a hand-drawn sketch and convert it into vector graphics so you can edit it in Illustrator. The Image Trace feature makes this very easy to do. After tracing it, you will add color and a background to make the graphic pop.

Tracing the Superhero Sketch

1. From the **Illustrator Class** folder, open the file **super hero.ai**.
2. Save as **yourname-the super hero.ai**, then hit **Save**.
3. In the dialog that appears, leave the default options checked and click **OK**.
4. Choose the **Selection** tool.
5. Go to **File > Place**.
6. Locate **super hero sketch.psd** and click **Place**.
7. **Click once** anywhere in the artboard to place the file at its actual size. (Do NOT click and drag, which will resize the file you're placing.)
8. Make sure it's still selected, and in the **Control** panel (at the top of the screen), click the **Align To** button and choose **Align to Artboard**.

3F Illustrator: Super Hero

9. Next to it, click the **Horizontal Align Center** button.
10. Also, click the **Vertical Align Center** button.
11. Still in the **Control** panel, click the **Image Trace** button.
12. The super hero scan has now been traced (converted to vectors) using the default options, but it's missing a lot of details. To customize the quality and settings, open the **Image Trace** panel (**Window > Image Trace**).
13. In the panel that opens, go to the bottom and make sure **Preview** is checked on.
14. At the top, set the **Preset** to **Sketched Art**.
15. In the **Image Trace** panel, click the triangle to the left of **Advanced** to see more options.
16. Set **Noise** to **1 px** and hit **Tab**. Notice how many lost details have reappeared.
17. Set **Threshold** to **180** and **Paths** to **90%** (hit **Tab** both times).
18. Click the **Trace** button to finish. (If **Trace** is not clickable, this means the Preview function has already updated the changes.)
19. In the **Control** panel, click the **Expand** button.

> **Image Trace**
>
> Once you are done tweaking the **Live Trace** options and have a nice vector drawing, you can do one of the following:
>
> - Do nothing, just leave the art in its current live state. This way, the **Image Trace** options can be tweaked later if needed.
> - Click the **Expand** button (in the **Control** panel) to render the vector outlines, so you can manually refine the art using standard tools. After expanding, you cannot tweak the **Image Trace** options.
> - After expanding, use the **Live Paint Bucket** tool to convert it into a Live Paint group.

Adding Some Color

1. Go to **Object > Live Paint > Make**. The image won't change but it got converted to a Live Paint Group, indicated by the starburst bounding box handles.
2. Deselect the artwork by clicking off of it.
3. Choose the **Live Paint Bucket** tool. If you don't see it, click and hold the **Shape Builder** tool.

Illustrator: Super Hero

3F

4. Notice the color swatches above the bucket cursor.

   NOTE: If you only see one color swatch above the cursor, click the **Properties** panel's **Fill** swatch to go into the **Swatches** panel. Then click on any swatch.

5. Press the **Left** and **Right Arrow** keys to cycle through the swatches.

6. Move the cursor over the superhero, but DO NOT click yet! Notice that fillable regions are outlined in bright red.

7. Use the Arrow keys to choose the proper swatch, then click on an outlined area to fill the superhero. Refer to the image and helpful tips below as a guide.

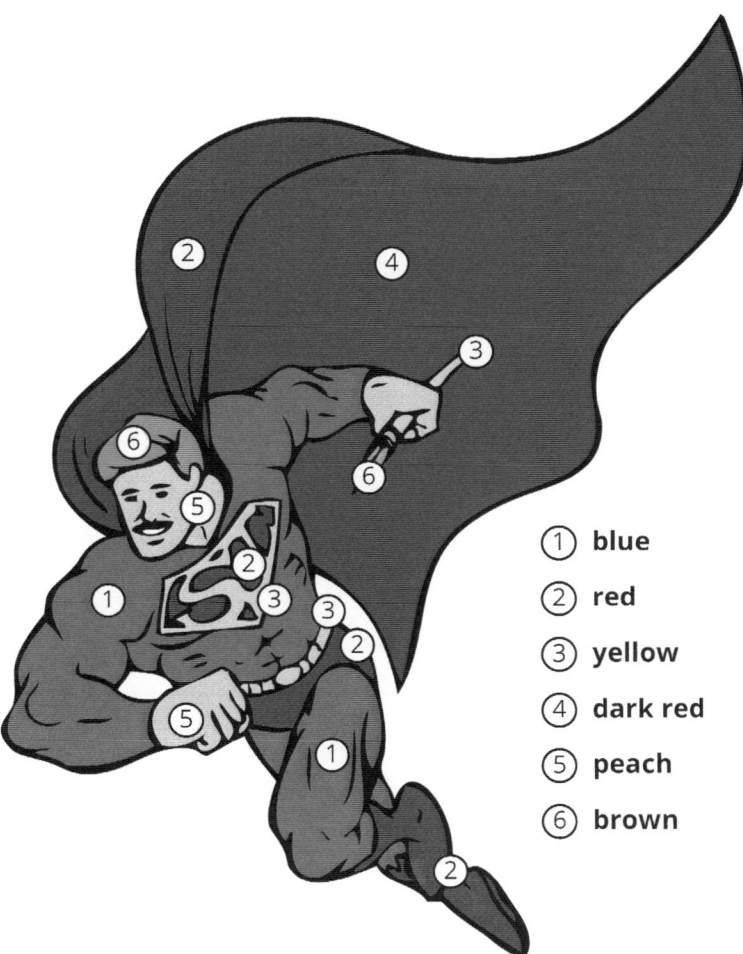

① blue
② red
③ yellow
④ dark red
⑤ peach
⑥ brown

- Be careful of the black strokes. These are actually fills that can be accidentally filled with another color. If you accidentally change them, just undo it.
- Don't forget to fill his teeth in with white!
- Zoom in to fill small areas that are hard to target.

3F Illustrator: Super Hero

Adding a Background

1. Go to **File > Place**.

2. In the **Illustrator Class** folder, locate **city sketch.psd** and click **Place**.

3. **Click once** on the left side of the artboard to place the file at its actual size. (Do NOT click and drag, which will resize the file you're placing.)

4. Choose the **Selection** tool.

5. Move the city sketch to the bottom of the document.

6. With the city sketch selected, go to the **Image Trace** panel and change the **Preset** to **Silhouettes**.

7. Under **Advanced** in the Image Trace panel, uncheck **Ignore White**.

8. In the **Control** panel or **Properties** panel, click the **Expand** button to turn it into editable artwork.

9. Click off the artwork to deselect it.

10. Choose the **Group Selection** tool. If you don't see it, click and hold the **Direct Selection** tool.

11. Select the white sky above the cityscape and press **Delete** to remove it.

12. Choose the **Selection** tool.

13. Select the cityscape again.

14. In the **Properties** panel under **Appearance**, click on the swatch next to **Fill**.

15. In the **Swatches** panel that opens, give it the **dark green** fill.

16. With the city still selected, go to **Object > Arrange > Send to Back**.

    The cityscape does not go behind the starburst because it is on a separate layer.

17. Select the **super hero**.

18. In the **Tools** panel, double-click the **Scale** tool.

19. Next to Uniform, enter a **Scale** of **110%** and click **OK**.

20. Choose the **Selection** tool and position him nicely in the center of the document, if he isn't already.

21. Press **Cmd–Shift–A** (Mac) or **Ctrl–Shift–A** (Windows) to deselect him.

Adding Finishing Touches

1. Select the **Paintbrush** tool.

Illustrator: Super Hero

2. Near the bottom of the **Properties** panel in the **Brush** section, click the **Brush Libraries** button (it's on the far right). From the menu, choose **Artistic > Artistic_Calligraphic**.

    NOTE: In CC 2017 and earlier, we would open the **Brushes** panel (**Window > Brushes**) to get to this button.

3. From the panel that opens, select the **5 pt. Oval**. If you're unsure which brush it is, go to the **Brush panel menu** and select **List View** to display all the available brushes listed by name.

4. In the **Properties** panel, change the **Stroke** to **black** and make sure **Fill** is set to none.

5. As shown below, use the **Paintbrush** tool to create a few action lines coming out of the hero's back to make it look like he's flying in to save the day.

6. When finished, close the **Artistic_Calligraphic** brush panel.

7. Choose the **Flare** tool. If you can't find the flare, click and hold on the **Rounded Rectangle** tool (or possibly the Rectangle tool).

8. At the back of the hero's belt, click and drag out a large solar flare. If you don't like the look of the flare, just undo and try it again.

9. Select **File > Save** and close the file. Super!

Illustrator: Juggling Colors & Gradients

Exercise Preview

Exercise Overview

This poster starts off as a plain grayscale graphic. You'll spice it up by adding colored strokes, fills, and gradients.

Coloring the Juggler's Body

1. In the **Illustrator Class** folder, open the file **Juggler.ai**.

2. This drawing is basically complete, but it needs color. Let's start by hitting the letter **D** on the keyboard to get the default white fill and black stroke.

3. Select the body of the juggler.

4. Using the **Properties** panel's **Color Mixer**, give it a **black fill** and a **1 pt black stroke**. Remember to press **Return** (Mac) or **Enter** (Windows) to close the panel.

5. Select the diamond pattern on the juggler's legs. Give it a **1 pt stroke** and set the color to **100c** and **39m** (and don't forget to set **0y** and **0k**).

    NOTE: If you don't see CMYK values for this and other color settings, go into the **panel menu** at the top right of the Color Mixer panel and choose **CMYK**.

3G Illustrator: Juggling Colors & Gradients

6. Select the design on the juggler's chest. You will need to click the **sternum** and then **Shift–click** to get the **ribs** too.

7. Make the color **75c**, **59y** and set the stroke to **none**.

8. **Shift–click** the **sternum** to deselect it so that only the **ribs** are selected.

9. You are now going to reduce the saturation of the color in the ribs. First, go to the **Properties** panel and click the **Fill** swatch.

10. Holding down the **Shift** key, slide the cyan portion of the color to approximately **45%**. The yellow will slide with it.

Coloring the Floor

1. The floor is composed of one background object and a group of diamond floor tiles in front. Select the background by clicking any of the darker areas on the floor.

2. Fill it with **20c, 5m, 5y, 10k**. (You may need to choose CMYK from the panel menu.)

3. We want to create a new CMYK color swatch, but first, click on the light diamond floor tiles (they're grouped).

4. Change the Fill color to **6c, 15y**.

5. Let's save this color as a swatch. Go into the **Color Mixer panel menu** and choose **Create New Swatch**.

6. In the dialog that opens:

    - Change the Swatch Name to **floor tiles**

    - Uncheck **Add to my Library**.

    NOTE: If we did not uncheck **Add to my Library**, this color would be saved into a shared library available for all files. We only want to use the color in this file.

7. Click **OK**.

8. Select the **shadows** behind or under the juggler's legs.

9. Fill them with **10c, 5m, 20k**.

10. With the shadows selected, go to the **Properties** panel's **Appearance** section and click on the word **Opacity** (not its checkered swatch!) to bring up the Transparency panel.

    NOTE: In CC 2017 and older, we would open the standalone **Transparency** panel by going to **Window > Transparency**.

11. In the **Transparency** panel, you'll see a menu that says **Normal**. Change this to **Multiply**. (This uses the shadow shape to darken the colors that are underneath, thus giving the look of a natural shadow.)

Illustrator: Juggling Colors & Gradients

12. To close the Transparency panel, press **Return** (Mac) or **Enter** (Windows).

Coloring the Juggler's Face

1. Zoom in and select the outline of the juggler's face.

2. In the **Properties** panel, click on the **Fill** swatch.

3. We've created some swatches for you ahead of time, including one for the skin. At the top middle of the Color Mixer panel, click the **Swatches** button to switch to the Swatches panel.

4. Near the top of the **Swatches** panel, make sure the **Find Field** is showing (next to a icon). If it is not, go into the **panel menu** in the top-right corner and choose **Show Find Field**.

5. In the **Find Field**, start typing in **skintone**. Illustrator will narrow down the options to display only the **skintone** swatch. Click on this swatch to apply it.

6. Click the **x** in the **Find Field** to clear the search.

7. To close the Swatches panel, press **Return** (Mac) or **Enter** (Windows).

8. Do a **Select > Deselect** (**Cmd–Shift–A** (Mac) or **Ctrl–Shift–A** (Windows)).

9. Select the juggler's lips and go to the **Properties** panel. Make sure it has no stroke, then click on the **Fill** swatch.

10. Let's create a custom color. At the bottom of the **Swatches** panel, click the **New Swatch** button.

11. In the **New Swatch** dialog that opens, enter the following:

    Swatch Name: **Bright Red**
    Color Type: **Process Color**
    Global: Check this option on
    Color Mode: **CMYK**
    Color: Mix a color that is **100m**, **50y**.
    Add to my Library: Uncheck this option

12. Click **OK**.

13. Hit **Cmd–Shift–A** (Mac) or **Ctrl–Shift–A** (Windows) to do a **Select > Deselect**.

14. Now you'll create some gradient fills. Open the **Gradient** panel by going to **Window > Gradient**.

15. At the bottom, click on the **Gradient Slider** to get the **color stops** to show.

3G Illustrator: Juggling Colors & Gradients

16. If there are more than two color stops, delete the extras by dragging them down and off the panel. Leave color stops at the beginning and end of the gradient slider so it looks as shown below:

17. Double–click the **left color stop** in the **Gradient** panel.

18. As shown below, click the **Swatches** button on the left of the pop-up panel to view the swatches.

    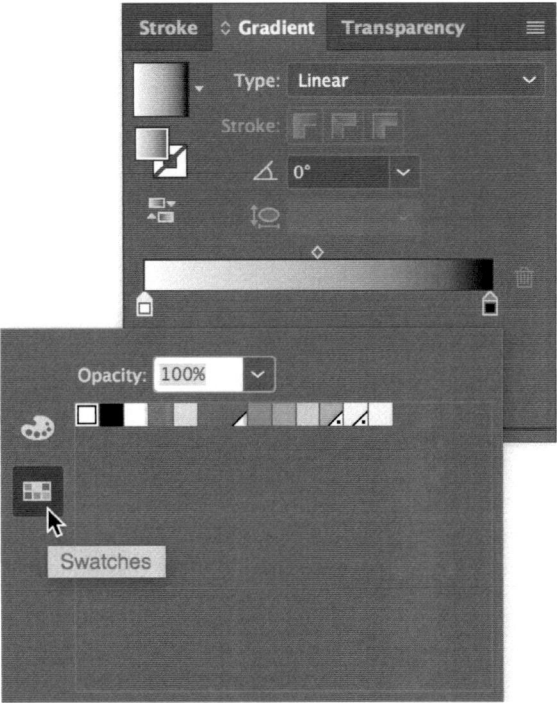

19. Select the **dull red** swatch (hover over a swatch to see its name).

20. Click the **Color** button on the left of the pop-up panel.

21. Change the **Tint (T)** of the dull red to **50%** and hit **Return** (Mac) or **Enter** (Windows).

22. Double–click the **right color stop** in the **Gradient** panel.

23. Click the **Swatches** button on the left, then select the **skintone** swatch.

24. Click on the **Gradient** panel to close the Swatches pop-up panel.

25. Near the top of the **Gradient** panel, make the Type: **Radial**. (If you don't see this option in the panel, go into the **panel menu** and choose **Show Options**.)

Illustrator: Juggling Colors & Gradients

26. Now that the gradient is done, we want to add it to the **Swatches** panel to save it. It's easiest to do that in the standalone Swatches panel that isn't tied to the Properties panel, so go to **Window > Swatches**.

27. At the bottom of the **Swatches** panel, click the **New Swatch** button.

    NOTE: Another option for creating a swatch is dragging a swatch from the **Gradient** panel and dropping it into the **Swatches** panel.

28. Name the new gradient swatch **cheek** and hit **OK**.

29. Make sure the **Fill** icon is active, and drag and drop the swatch onto the circle of the juggler's cheek.

Coloring the Juggling Balls

1. Select the top juggling ball.

2. In the **Swatches** panel, fill the ball with the **yellow to red** gradient (it's already been created for you).

3. Let's change the direction of the gradient. Make sure the ball is selected and choose the **Gradient** tool in the **Tools** panel.

4. Drag from the upper left of the ball (just outside of it) down to the lower right.

5. Let's copy this colored gradient so you can apply it to the other balls. Double–click the **Eyedropper** tool to see its options.

6. At the top, we want **Appearance** to be checked on in BOTH columns. If it's not checked on, do so now. Click **OK**.

7. Do a **Select > Deselect**.

8. Use the **Selection** tool to select the two lower juggling balls, holding the **Shift** key to get both.

9. Select the **Eyedropper** tool.

10. Click on the gradient ball to sample its appearance.

    The other two juggling balls are filled with the gradient. Note that the direction and placement of the gradient stays the same too!

11. Do a **Select > Deselect** (**Cmd–Shift–A** (Mac) or **Ctrl–Shift–A** (Windows)).

12. You are now going to edit a gradient. At the top left of the **Gradient** panel, next to the Gradient thumbnail, click the arrow to bring up a list of gradient swatches.

13. Select the **yellow to red** gradient swatch.

3G Illustrator: Juggling Colors & Gradients

14. In the area just below the gradient slider, click anywhere between the **start** and **end color stops**. This will create a new stop.

15. Drag the new color stop until the **Location** number is approximately **80%**, or just type **80%** in the Location field.

16. Double–click the new color stop.

17. Click the **Color** button on the left and change this color to **74m, 50y**.

18. Double–click the **last color stop** on the right.

19. Add **28c** to its existing CMYK values and hit **Return** (Mac) or **Enter** (Windows).

    You created a gradient that goes from yellow to red to a darker version of the red.

20. To create a new gradient swatch, go to the bottom of the **Swatches** panel and click the **New Swatch** button.

21. In the dialog that appears, name it **juggling balls** and click **OK**.

22. Drag the new swatch over the juggling balls in the image to change their gradients.

Styling the Hair & Juggling Line

1. Using the **Selection** tool, click on a strand of the juggler's hair. (All of the hairs should become selected because they are grouped.)

2. Zoom in on it so you can see the changes we make.

3. In the **Properties** panel, change the hair to have a stroke of **1.5 pt black**.

4. With the hair selected, go to the **Properties** panel's **Appearance** section and click on the word **Stroke** (not its swatch!) to bring up the Stroke panel.

5. In the **Stroke** panel, change the Cap to **Round Cap**.

6. To close the Stroke panel, click in a blank area outside of it.

7. Zoom out a bit and select the black line between the juggler's hands.

8. Reopen the **Stroke** panel (by going to the Properties panel and clicking on the word).

9. In the **Stroke** panel, check the **Dashed Line** option.

10. Type **4** above the **first dash** field and **6** above the **first gap** field. Hit **Return** (Mac) or **Enter** (Windows) to apply it.

11. With the dashed line still selected, set its **Stroke** color to **Bright Red**. (Switch to the **Swatches** if you don't see this.)

12. Press **Cmd–Shift–A** (Mac) or **Ctrl–Shift–A** (Windows) to deselect and see the effect.

Illustrator: Juggling Colors & Gradients

Coloring the Background & Text

1. Select the box around the juggler.

2. Give it a **3.5 pt black** stroke, and **Fill** it with **61c, 30m, 6y, 10k**.

3. Go down to the text underneath the juggler. Select the word **MILANO**.

4. In the **Swatches** panel, fill the letters with the **yellow to dk blue** gradient.

5. Use the **Gradient** tool to play with the direction of the blend. Drag over the type to change the gradient's angle and length.

   NOTE: You'll notice that at first the gradient blend occurs once in each letter, but if you use the **Gradient** tool while all the letters are selected, it will sweep the gradient fill across all of the letters at once.

6. Finally, using the **Gradient** tool, hold **Shift** (to ensure the gradient will be straight up and down) and drag from the **M's top** to its **bottom**.

7. Hey, that's pretty nice. **Save** your file as **yourname-juggler.ai** and you're done!

   NOTE: If you get an alert about spot colors and transparency, just click **Continue**. This is just a warning that converting the file to process colors outside of Illustrator can cause unexpected results. We won't be doing that, so it's not a problem.

Illustrator: Combining Shapes with the Pathfinder

3H

Exercise Preview

Exercise Overview

The Pathfinder is an excellent way to create shapes and special effects. Instead of drawing the woman by hand, you will cut, overlap, and merge various shapes to create the finished illustration shown above.

1. From the **Illustrator Class** folder, open the file **geisha.ai**.

2. Make sure the **Pathfinder** panel is open (go to **Window > Pathfinder** if it's not open).

Creating/Assembling the Illustration

You will see an assortment of shapes. Many of these shapes have been created by modifying ellipses using the **Direct Selection** and **Anchor Point** tools. You'll use the Pathfinder panel to combine them to create more complex shapes that would have been harder to make if you had to draw the final shapes yourself.

1. First we'll create the hairline. With the **Selection** tool, drag the **Slice Line** over the **Large Oval**. Refer to the example for correct placement.

3H Illustrator: Combining Shapes with the Pathfinder

2. Make sure some of the slice line hangs slightly off the edge of the hair at the bottom.

3. With the line still selected, go to **Object > Path > Divide Objects Below**. This will cut the object into two pieces using the slice line as a guide.

4. We don't need the smaller piece we've created. Go to **Select > Deselect**.

5. Select and **delete** that slice by-product so you are left with just the shape of the hair.

6. Move the **hairpiece** over the **face** shape and contemplate a new career in digital hairdressing. Be a good hairdresser and make sure there are no little white spaces showing through.

7. **Shift–click** on the face so that both the hair and the face are selected.

8. In the **Pathfinder** panel (Window > Pathfinder), under **Pathfinders**, click the **Trim** button . This makes the face into a shape that doesn't include the part obscured by the hair.

9. The face and the hair are now grouped but we don't need them to stay grouped. Choose **Object > Ungroup**.

10. Select the piece labeled **Hair Bun** and drag it so it partially protrudes from the top right of the hair.

11. Hold **Shift** and **click** on the hair to add it to your selection (you should have both black objects selected).

12. In the **Pathfinder** panel, under Shape Modes, **Opt–click** (Mac) or **Alt–click** (Windows) the **Unite** button to add the two shapes together. It may not look like anything has happened, but give us a second to prove it.

13. With the hair still selected, give it:

    - A **3 pt stroke** with a color of **15c, 35m, 100y**.

    - A fill color of **35c, 85m, 85y, 75k**.

    NOTE: If you don't see CMYK values, go to the **panel menu** and select **CMYK**.

14. Deselect it so you can see how Illustrator now sees the hair as one shape!

15. You can still move the bun separately. Choose the **Group Selection** tool .

Illustrator: Combining Shapes with the Pathfinder   3H

16. Make sure only the bun circle is selected. Then move it around and see how the whole thing still looks as though it's one shape.

> **The Pathfinder Panel**
>
> By default, the Shape Modes will automatically merge multiple paths into a single path. To make a compound path (in which all the paths are maintained as distinct and editable objects), you must **Opt–click** (Mac) or **Alt–click** (Windows) one of the Shape Mode buttons in the Pathfinder panel.

17. This looks good so far, but our lady is earless. Using the **Selection** tool, drag the piece labeled **Ear** into a position appropriate for an ear. Refer to the example if you have to.

18. **Shift–click** on the **face** and in the **Pathfinder** panel, under Shape Modes, click the **Unite** button.

19. Drag the **Eyebrows** and **Lips** onto the face and position them properly.

20. Drag the **Fan** over so it is partially obscuring her lips.

21. Deselect the fan.

22. With the **Group Selection** tool, click on the **orange** part of the **fan**.

23. In the **Properties** panel or the **Control** panel at the top of the screen, set the **Opacity** to **70%**.

24. Select the entire Geisha and do an **Object > Group**.

    This part of the drawing is complete!

25. Select **File > Save As** and name it **yourname-geisha.ai**.

    NOTE: If you get an alert about spot colors and transparency, click **Continue**.

Moving the Illustration onto a Cover

1. Select the **Geisha** and copy her (**Cmd–C** (Mac) or **Ctrl–C** (Windows)).

2. Open the **MenuCover.ai** file.

3. Switch to the **Layers** panel by clicking its name in the tabs at the top right.

4. In the **Layers panel menu** make sure **Paste Remembers Layers** is **NOT** checked. If it is checked, choose it to turn it off.

5. Paste the illustration (**Cmd–V** (Mac) or **Ctrl–V** (Windows)).

6. Position it into the red area.

3H Illustrator: Combining Shapes with the Pathfinder

7. Scale the Geisha **90%** (double–click the **Scale** tool and enter the amount next to **Uniform**).

8. You're done! Save the file as **yourname-MenuCover.ai**.

9. In the dialog that appears, leave the default options checked and click **OK**.

   In the future, keep in mind that sometimes you can build an illustration more effectively than drawing it from scratch!
   # Exercise **4A**: Final Project: Sporktown Brochure

Exercise Preview

 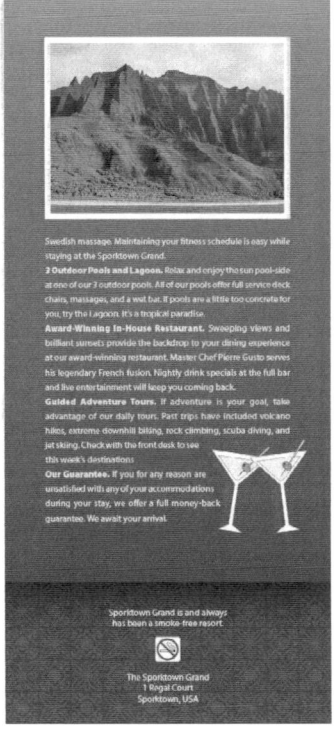

Exercise Overview

In this exercise, you'll create a hotel brochure. We'll show you how to place multiple graphics, link text from one page to another, and set text wrap, as well as how to handle bleed and strokes.

Illustrator: Combining Shapes with the Pathfinder   3H

Creating the Document

1. Go to **File > New > Document** and set the following:

   - Set Width to **4 in** and Height to **9 in**.
   - If the number of **Pages** and the **Start #** aren't already **1**, change them now.
   - Uncheck **Facing Pages**.
   - Expand the **Margins** section if needed, and make all Margins **0.5 in**.
   - Expand the **Bleed and Slug** section if needed, and make all Bleed options **0.125 in**.

2. Click **Create**.
3. In the **InDesign CC** menu (Mac) or **Edit** menu (Windows), choose **Preferences** and then **Units & Increments**.
4. Change both **Horizontal** and **Vertical** to **Picas**. Click **OK**.
5. Go to **File > Save As** and name it **yourname-sporktown-grand.indd**.

Laying Out the Backgrounds

1. Go into **File > Place**.
2. From the **InDesign Class** folder, then the **Sporktown Brochure** folder, select **background-pattern.ai** and click **Open**.

   The cursor is now a loaded image icon with a preview of the background.

3. Position the top left of this cursor at the **red bleed guide** (which is ⅛ **in** off the top left of the page) and click **once** to place the background.
4. Choose the **Rectangle Frame** tool.
5. Click and drag a rectangle from the top left bleed to the bottom right bleed.
6. In the **Control** panel, click the **bottom center** reference point.
7. Enter an **H** (Height) of **46p4** and press **Return** (Mac) or **Enter** (Windows) to make the change.
8. Make sure the rectangle is still selected.
9. Open the **Swatches** panel (**Window > Color > Swatches**).
10. As shown below, at the top left of the **Swatches** panel, make sure the **Fill** swatch is in front (active). If it's not, click it to make it active.

3H Illustrator: Combining Shapes with the Pathfinder

11. Now we can create a gradient swatch. From the **Swatches panel menu** at the top right, choose **New Gradient Swatch**.

12. Enter the following:

    Swatch Name: **text background**
            Type: **Linear**

13. In the **Gradient Ramp** section, click on the left slider to select it.

14. Make sure the **Stop Color** is set to CMYK and set the color: **48% Cyan, 47% Magenta, 60% Yellow, 16% Black**.

15. In the **Gradient Ramp** section, click on the right slider to select it.

16. Make sure the **Stop Color** is set to CMYK and set the color: **63% Cyan, 62% Magenta, 67% Yellow, 57% Black**.

17. Click **OK**.

18. Let's change the direction of the gradient. Make sure the rectangle is still selected.

19. Choose the **Gradient Swatch** tool.

20. Hold **Shift** and **drag** from the top of the rectangle to the bottom.

21. Go to **Object > Effects > Drop Shadow**.

22. Check on **Preview** and set the following:

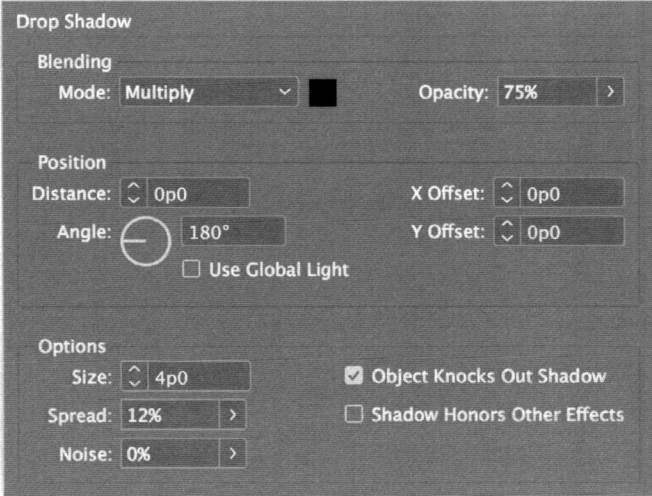

23. Click **OK**.

24. Open the **Pages** panel (**Window > Pages**).

25. Select **page 1**.

Illustrator: Combining Shapes with the Pathfinder   3H

26. Hold **Option** (Mac) or **Alt** (Windows) and drag **page 1** down, then let go to make a copy of the page as shown below.

    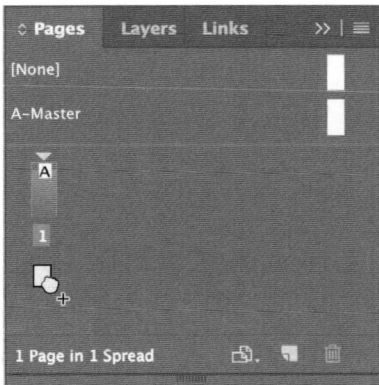

27. Choose the **Selection** tool.

28. On **page 2**, move the gradient box up to the top of the bleed guide.

29. In the **Control** panel, select the **top left** reference point.

30. In the **Control** panel, change the **H** (Height) to **44p3** to make it a little shorter.

Making the Front Page

1. Scroll up to **page 1**.

2. Click in the empty space off the page to make sure nothing is selected.

3. Go to **File > Place**.

4. From the **Sporktown Brochure** folder, double–click **Sporktown-grand-logo.ai**.

5. The cursor should now have the image loaded. Click once, slightly off the top edge of the page, to place the logo.

6. Now let's perfect the position of the logo. Mouse over the image and notice (don't click) the circle that appears in the center of the image (which is called the **content grabber**).

   An image in InDesign consists of a frame and the image inside the frame. You can use the **Selection** tool to either move the frame and the image, or adjust the position of the image inside the frame. The content grabber is used to move the image inside of the frame. Clicking anywhere on the image except for the content grabber allows you to move the image and the frame together.

3H Illustrator: Combining Shapes with the Pathfinder

7. Using the **Selection** tool , click anywhere on the logo except for the content grabber in the center, and move it so the bottom of the spork sits near the top of the gradient rectangle and centered between the margins, as shown below.

   NOTE: Almost half the spork should be cut off at the top of the page.

8. Let's make sure the spork is centered horizontally. With the logo still selected, hold **Shift** and click on the pattern.

9. Open the **Align** panel (**Window > Object & Layout > Align**).

10. Click the button next to **Align To** and from the menu choose **Align to Selection**.

11. Click the **Align horizontal centers** button .

12. Click on the pasteboard off to the side to deselect all.

13. Press **Cmd–D** (Mac) or **Ctrl–D** (Windows), which is the keystroke for **File > Place**.

14. From the **Sporktown Brochure** folder, choose **hotel-exterior.tif**.

15. Click once off the left side of the page, but make sure you don't accidentally click into the gradient rectangle!

16. Enter **X: –0p9** and **Y: 14p3**

Making the Back Page

1. Scroll to **page 2**.

2. Click on the pasteboard off the left side to make sure nothing is selected.

3. Go to **File > Place**.

Illustrator: Combining Shapes with the Pathfinder 3H

4. Hold **Cmd** (Mac) or **Ctrl** (Windows), and select the following three files:

    - **coastline.psd**
    - **martinis.ai**
    - **no-smoking.ai**

5. Click **Open**.

6. The files are now loaded in the cursor next to a **3** and a preview of the **current file**. The number shows how many images are loaded to place. The currently loaded image should be the **coastline** photo (press any Arrow key until it is).

7. Click once **off the left side** of the page to place the photo.

8. The cursor should now display (2) and show a preview of the martinis image.

9. Click once **off the right side** of the page to store the martinis for later use.

10. Click once **slightly off the bottom** of the page to place the **no-smoking sign**.

11. Move the **no-smoking sign** upwards so it's in the middle of the pattern section.

12. Move the **coastline** photo to the top of the page, fitting into the margin guides.

Bringing in the Text

To save time, we've typed and styled all the text for you in another InDesign file.

1. Go to **File > Open** and choose the InDesign file **Sporktown-text.indd** from the **Sporktown Brochure** folder.

2. Choose the **Type** tool.

3. Click inside the **top** text frame and select all (**Cmd–A** (Mac) or **Ctrl–A** (Windows)).

4. Copy it (**Cmd–C** (Mac) or **Ctrl–C** (Windows)).

5. Switch back to the **yourname-sporktown-grand** file.

6. Go to **page 1**.

7. Inside the margin guides below the photo, click and drag a box following the margin guides to the bottom of the page (purple guide). Leave some space between the photo and text.

8. Paste the text (**Cmd–V** (Mac) or **Ctrl–V** (Windows)).

9. Notice the red text overflow symbol on the bottom right of the text frame. That means there's too much text to fit inside this box. We want the extra text to flow from this box to the back page.

10. Go down to **page 2**.

Illustrator: Combining Shapes with the Pathfinder

11. Inside the margin guides below the photo, click and drag another text box following the guides to the end of the gradient box (blue guide).

12. Go back up to **page 1**.

13. Choose the **Selection** tool .

14. Click directly on the text overflow symbol . The cursor will load up a preview of that box's text. (If you don't see the cursor loaded with text, try clicking it again.)

15. Scroll down to **page 2**.

16. Position the cursor over the text box you just created, and when it changes into a chain , click to link the boxes. The text should flow freely from page 1 to 2.

17. Switch back to the **Sporktown-text** file. If you closed it earlier, open it again.

18. Choose the **Type** tool .

19. Select the text (not the box) at the bottom of the page.

20. Copy it (**Cmd–C** (Mac) or **Ctrl–C** (Windows)).

21. Switch back to the **yourname-sporktown-grand** file.

22. Make sure that you are on **page 2**.

23. At the bottom of the page, click and drag a new text box filling the margins over the pattern (a little bit below the gradient).

24. Paste the text (**Cmd–V** (Mac) or **Ctrl–V** (Windows)) into the box.

Text Wrap

The text is covering over the no-smoking graphic at the bottom. Fortunately we can easily fix that with text wrap.

1. Choose the **Selection** tool .

2. Try to select the no-smoking image. If the text is on top of the image, you'll find that you can't click to select the image beneath.

3. Hold **Cmd** (Mac) or **Ctrl** (Windows) and click on the no-smoking image.

   NOTE: Holding **Cmd** (Mac) or **Ctrl** (Windows) lets you click through boxes to whatever is underneath. It might take a few clicks to select the no-smoking sign.

4. Go to **Object > Arrange > Bring to Front** to move it in front.

5. Open the **Text Wrap** panel (**Window > Text Wrap**).

6. At the top of the panel, click the **Jump object** button .

   This will make the text jump to the line below the image.

Illustrator: Combining Shapes with the Pathfinder

7. Make the text frame taller; it's OK that it goes below the bottom margin guide.

8. Position the no-smoking sign so that the text jumps after "**smoke-free resort**."

9. The no-smoking sign is too large. Do the following:

    - Click once on the sign to select it.

    - Hold **Cmd–Shift** (Mac) or **Ctrl–Shift** (Windows).

    - Position the cursor over the bottom right resize handle.

    - Click and hold for about 2 seconds before you move the mouse to resize the graphic.

    - Resize it down to roughly ¾ the size of a pattern element.

    TIP: Holding the mouse down for a bit before you move it lets you see a live preview of the image, otherwise you just see the bounding box. Holding **Cmd** (Mac) or **Ctrl** (Windows) lets you resize the box and the image inside at the same time.

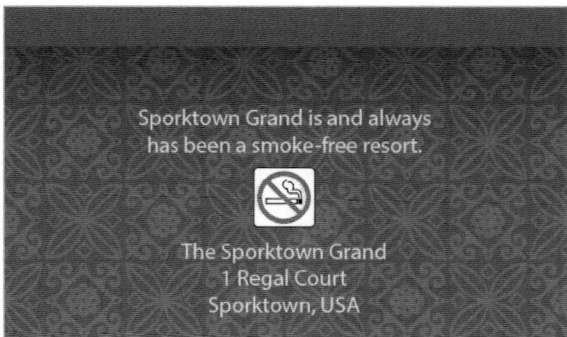

10. With the no-smoking sign selected, **Shift–click** the surrounding text to select it too.

11. Visually center it between the top and the bottom of the pattern area.

12. Go to **Window > Object & Layout > Align**.

13. As shown below, click the button next to **Align To** and from the menu choose **Align to Page**.

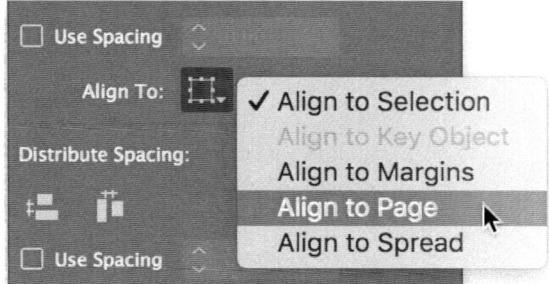

14. Click the **Align horizontal centers** button to make sure everything is centered in the middle of the page.

3H Illustrator: Combining Shapes with the Pathfinder

15. On the pasteboard, select the martinis.

16. Go to **Object > Arrange > Bring to Front** so we can easily select them in the future (they were created earlier and therefore would be behind the text).

17. Move them over the lower-right corner of the body text.

18. Open the **Text Wrap** panel (**Window > Text Wrap**).

19. At the top of the panel, click the third button **Wrap around object shape** .

20. Set the remaining options as shown:

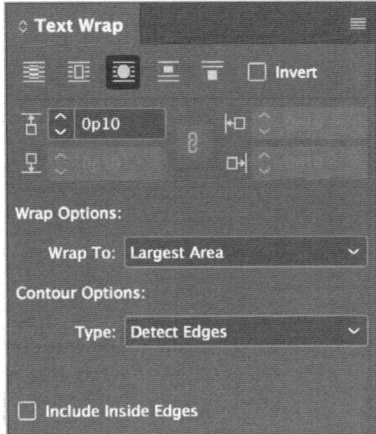

NOTE: Choosing **Detect Edges** wraps the text around the edges of the artwork, not the box.

21. Move the martinis around until you get it looking nice. You should be able to get everything fitting together nicely as shown.

22. Press **W** to switch into Preview mode and enjoy your work.

23. Save your work.

Illustrator: Combining Shapes with the Pathfinder 3H

Bonus Goodies (If You Have Extra Time)

1. Press **W** to switch back to **Normal** mode.

2. Go to **page 1**.

3. Choose the **Type** tool.

4. Below the **Sporktown Grand** logo, click and drag a box from margin to margin.

5. Go to **Type > Glyphs**.

   NOTE: The Glyphs panel shows all the available characters for any given font.

6. At the bottom left of the **Glyphs** panel, from the font menu, choose **Wingdings**.

7. Scroll down until you locate the **star** ★ and double-click it. You should see the star appear in the text box. (If you can't find the star, make sure the Show menu at the top says **Entire Font**.)

8. In the **Glyphs** panel, double-click the star **three** more times to have **four** stars in total.

9. Select the stars.

10. In the **Control** panel, **center** the stars and make them size **14 pt**.

11. Open the **Swatches** panel (**Window > Color > Swatches**).

12. Give them the **light brown** color swatch.

13. Choose the **Selection** tool.

14. Select the **hotel exterior** photo.

15. In the **Control** panel, make the Stroke weight **2 pt**.

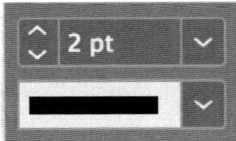

16. In the **Swatches** panel, make sure the **stroke** swatch is in front. If it's not, click it to make it active.

17. We want the stroke to be the same color as the logo's stroke, but we don't have that color yet. From the **Swatches panel menu** at the top right, choose **New Color Swatch**.

3H Illustrator: Combining Shapes with the Pathfinder

18. Leave **Name with Color Value** checked and set the following:

    Color Type: **Process**
    Color Mode: **CMYK**
    Color Values: **47% Cyan**, **67% Magenta**, **78% Yellow**, **55% Black**
    Add to CC Library: Uncheck this option if shown

    NOTE: If you completed the previous exercise, InDesign should remember that you don't want to add this swatch to a CC Library.

19. Click **OK**.

20. Open the **Stroke** panel (**Window > Stroke**).

21. The stroke doesn't quite go off the edge of our bleed, so for safety's sake, click the **Align Stroke to Outside** button.

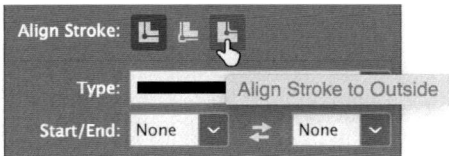

22. Go to **page 2**.

23. Select the **coastline** photo.

24. Open the **Swatches** panel.

25. Make sure the **stroke** icon is active and give it a **[Paper]** color stroke.

26. Open the **Stroke** panel.

27. Give it a **5 pt** stroke.

28. As shown below, click the **Align Stroke to Inside** button.

29. Go into **View > Display Performance** and make sure **High Quality Display** is checked on.

30. Take a look at the pattern at the bottom. Notice that it doesn't quite line up perfectly in the corners?

31. Select the pattern.

32. Move it down until the pattern's squares fit perfectly into the corners, like they do on the top of page 1.

33. Press **W** to switch into Preview mode and enjoy your work.

Illustrator: Combining Shapes with the Pathfinder

34. Save your work.

    That's it! You've mastered this piece.

    ___

Check Out
OUR OTHER WORKBOOKS!

Web Development Level 1 and 2

JavaScript & jQuery

GreenSock Animation

Mobile & Responsive Web Design

WordPress

PHP & MySQL

Ruby on Rails

Photoshop for Web & UI

Photoshop Animated GIFs

Adobe Experience Design

Sketch

HTML Email

Responsive HTML Email

PowerPoint

Adobe InDesign

Adobe Illustrator

Adobe Photoshop

Photoshop Advanced

Adobe Lightroom

Adobe After Effects

Adobe CC: Intro to InDesign, Photoshop, & Illustrator

NOBLEDESKTOP.COM/BOOKS